DR DOREL IOSIF

The Leadership Challenge Reimagined

Harnessing Energy and Advancing Human Progress

Copyright © 2025 by Dr Dorel Iosif

All rights reserved. No part of this publication may be reproduced, stored or transmitted in any form or by any means, electronic, mechanical, photocopying, recording, scanning, or otherwise without written permission from the publisher. It is illegal to copy this book, post it to a website, or distribute it by any other means without permission.

This novel is entirely a work of fiction. The names, characters and incidents portrayed in it are the work of the author's imagination. Any resemblance to actual persons, living or dead, events or localities is entirely coincidental.

Dr Dorel Iosif asserts the moral right to be identified as the author of this work.

First edition

ISBN: 978-0-646-71424-0

Aaron and Honor

To Honor, your love, strength, and unwavering support have been my greatest sources of inspiration.
To Aaron, my greatest pride, may you always chase your dreams with courage and integrity.
This book is for you, with all my love.

Contents

Prologue — 1
Introduction — 3

I Leadership and Innovation

1 A Short Saga of Human Progress — 9
2 Decision by Convergence — 25
3 Innovation from Galileo to DARPA — 45

II Energy - Navigating Disruption

4 A Short History of Energy Transitions — 69
5 Energy Transitions – A Story of Leadership and Betrayal — 90
6 The Evolution of the Hydrogen Economy — 113
7 Jevons' Paradox - The Future of AI and Computing — 136

III Integrity and the Corporate Culture

8 The Value of Integrity in Leadership — 159
9 The Curious Case of Corporate Culture – A Satire — 175

IV The Path Forward – Leadership in Action

10	The EU's New AI Act: Leading the AI Regulation	195
11	Toward Net Zero and Beyond	210

Epilogue   222

Prologue

Embarking on the journey of writing this book felt much like weaving a vast and intricate tapestry. Each article I'd previously written was a thread, a fragment of thought nestled at the intersection of strategy, leadership, energy transitions, and philosophy. Bringing them together into a coherent whole seemed, at times, an insurmountable challenge.

The genesis of this book lies in a deep desire to link together narratives and insights that have shaped my understanding of leadership and progress. Each chapter stands on the foundation of countless hours of research, reflection, and writing, embodying a unique intersection of historical precedent, modern challenges, and philosophical musings. These musings often stem from my love of philosophy and profound conversations with my son, whose insightful questions and perspectives continually inspire me and push the boundaries of my thinking.

Writing this book has been a monumental task, but one that has reaffirmed my belief in strategic leadership's power and the importance of thoughtful, informed decision-making. I hope this book serves as a guide and a source of inspiration for current and future leaders navigating our rapidly changing world. If, along the way, you find a nugget of wisdom or a spark of inspiration, then every ounce of effort has been worth it.

In the end, leadership, much like philosophy, is about questioning, exploring, and never settling for easy answers. It is about embracing monumental tasks and perhaps, in that pursuit, finding our true calling.

Introduction

Throughout the annals of human history, from the primordial blaze kindled in ancient caves to the sophisticated AI-driven transformations of the modern era, one elemental force has remained unwavering: leadership. It stands as the unseen orchestrator of strategy, the silent bastion of trust, and the catalytic spark that transmutes mere ideas into tangible action. As we delve into this narrative, it becomes abundantly clear that leadership is not merely an adjunct to progress; it is its very heartbeat.

This tome is not solely concerned with energy, strategy, or innovation in isolation. Rather, it surveys the grand tapestry of human advancement, examining the vital roles played by leaders, thinkers, and visionaries who have indelibly shaped our world and continue to influence the choices we face today. Imagine, if you will, a mosaic of interwoven concepts where energy transitions, strategic foresight, artificial intelligence, and governance are not disparate elements, but rather integral components of the intricate puzzle of leadership.

Understanding history, therefore, becomes paramount. It is the lens through which we can discern the patterns of leadership that have driven human progress. By examining the past, we glean insights into the enduring qualities and decisions that have propelled societies forward. History serves not merely as a record of events but as a repository of invaluable lessons, offering us the wisdom of those who have navigated the tumultuous waters of change before us.

In our exploration of leadership, we shall uncover why integrity stands as a non-negotiable trait. It is the bedrock upon which trust is built, the foundation that supports the edifice of leadership. Without integrity, leadership crumbles into mere facade, devoid of substance and incapable of engendering genuine progress. We will delve into the narratives of individuals who have embodied this virtue, whose steadfastness and honesty have forged paths through uncertainty and adversity.

Energy transitions, too, will be examined not merely as technological evolutions but as epic battles of vision and resolve. These shifts are not just about adopting new technologies but about envisioning a future and steadfastly pursuing it, despite the myriad challenges that arise. The leaders who have championed these transitions have done so with a clarity of purpose and an unwavering commitment to their ideals, reminding us that true progress demands both innovation and tenacity.

In the realm of artificial intelligence, the choices we make today in governance, ethical frameworks, and cultural integration will undeniably shape the future landscape. AI represents a frontier where the principles of leadership are tested anew. It calls for leaders who can balance technological advancement with ethical considerations, ensuring that AI serves as a tool for enhancing human potential rather than diminishing it. The stories of those who have pioneered in this field will illuminate the path forward, offering both cautionary tales and inspiring narratives.

The narrative journey through this book will weave together

the stories of historical figures like Plato, Aristotle, and Kant whose philosophies have left indelible marks on the world. Their experiences provide a rich tapestry of insights, illustrating how leadership transcends time and context to offer lessons that are as relevant today as they were in their own eras.

Ultimately, this book seeks to craft a compelling narrative that marries history, science, and leadership philosophy into a cohesive exploration of human progress. It invites readers to not only reflect upon the past but to engage actively with the present and future. In understanding the interconnectedness of these elements, we are better equipped to navigate the complexities of our modern world, making choices that resonate with integrity, foresight, and a commitment to the greater good. Through this journey, we aim to inspire a new generation of leaders who will continue to shape the course of human history with wisdom and vision.

My goal is not to prescribe rigid frameworks, but to challenge thinking – to spark conversations, to offer perspectives, and to remind us that in the face of disruption, great leadership is not about knowing all the answers but about asking the right questions.

Let's begin.

I

Leadership and Innovation

1

A Short Saga of Human Progress

Throughout the expansive sweep of human history, every generation has witnessed a painstaking, delicate interplay among visionary leadership, technological breakthroughs, and the collective will of society - a relationship so intricate that it has defined and redefined the very notion of progress. Indeed, from the primal moment when early humans first learned to harness the mysterious power of fire, to the dizzying horizon of artificial intelligence that promises to reshape our existence, each monumental leap forward has been crafted not solely by the relentless march of invention, but by individuals who dared to challenge established norms, risk everything in the name of change, and broaden the boundaries of what might be deemed possible.

At its core, what exactly constitutes progress? Is it measured by the burgeoning accumulation of wealth, or perhaps by the relentless expansion of empires? Might it be found in the unyielding pursuit of modern innovation regardless of cost? For many luminaries of thought, particularly the ancient philosopher Aristotle, progress was not a matter of material accumulation or territorial conquest; it was fundamentally connected to the idea of eudaimonia - a state of flourishing that transcends mere survival, where both individuals and societies achieve their highest potential through the cultivation of virtue, reason, and meaningful purpose. Through this lens, progress can be re-assessed: Are the great societal metamorphoses, the leaps in technology and transformative upheavals in social organization, truly leading us toward more fulfilling, righteous lives? Or do we risk mistaking superficial growth for genuine advancement? These questions compel us to take a deeper look at the forces that have shaped our history and continue to guide our future.

The narrative of progress does not begin within the sterile confines of modern boardrooms, nor does it originate in the gleaming laboratories of cutting-edge research. Instead, it is rooted in the elemental experiences of our earliest ancestors, gathered around flickering fires in dim, shadowed caves. In these primordial settings, leadership was an entirely different concept. It was not the exercise of unyielding control or authoritarian might; it was a delicate act of guidance, an unspoken covenant built on the foundation of trust, respect, and mutual dependence. Consider the leader of a Paleolithic hunting party, whose authority was not derived from blunt command but through the ability to inspire confidence, coordinate complex strategies tailored to the capricious rhythms of nature, and ultimately ensure the survival of the entire group. It was more than a question of who led - the true measure was in how that leader harmonised individual efforts into a cohesive force fighting against the unforgiving wilderness.

As humanity evolved, so too did the means by which we exerted our influence over the environment. The rudimentary element of fire gave way to primitive tools, tangible symbols of our desire to master the natural world. These early tools gradually became the bedrock of agriculture, which in turn laid the foundations for civilization itself. Every tiny step forward - from the invention of the plow to the establishment of irrigation systems - was not merely a scientific or technological advance; each was an act of profound transformation in the ways humans organized themselves, governed their societies, and exercised leadership. Ancient Mesopotamian city-states emerged as the crucibles of early political organization. In these early societies, the role of leadership was both celebrated and feared; while visionary leaders sought to unlock human potential and foster a thriving community, others exploited their positions to enforce rigid hierarchies, stifling creativity and human development through despotism. Such dichotomies would persist as defining themes in the saga of human progress.

The dawn of civilisation marked an era of establishing order and societal norms. Yet, as centuries turned and the pendulum of progress swung, the desire to overthrow established orders became a potent force. The Renaissance and later the Industrial Revolution stand as emphatic examples of eras when the established order was questioned and, in many cases, shattered. Imagine the atmosphere of the Renaissance - a period where intellectual freedom reached unprecedented heights. Figures such as Leonardo da Vinci, Nicolaus Copernicus, and Galileo Galilei boldly challenged age-old dogmas and heralded a new age of inquiry. With defiant resolve, Galileo, facing the immense weight of the orthodox beliefs held by the most powerful institutions of his time, argued that the Earth was not the unassailable center of the universe. His courageous defiance, which led to vehement persecution and personal trials, eventually laid the groundwork for the scientific revolution - a testament to Aristotle's enduring argument that the relentless pursuit of truth is not merely an optional endeavor but the highest calling of humanity.

The very nature of leadership began to evolve dramatically as well. With the advent of the Industrial Revolution, leadership transcended intellectual and scientific pursuits and took on an entirely new dimension: it began to harness not just the power of human thought but also the might of machine and industry. The industrial titans of this era, such as James Watt and Henry Ford, were celebrated not merely as engineers or inventors but as brilliant strategists who orchestrated an entirely new economic reality. However, beneath the surface of this revolutionary progress lay the seeds of enduring challenges. The rapid development of industry and technology brought with it soaring inequalities, environmental degradation, and the systematic exploitation of labor. The gleam of technological marvels was shadowed by the grim realities of dehumanised production lines where workers were often reduced to little more than components in a vast, mechanistic process - each individual's well-being frequently sacrificed on the altar of efficiency and profit.

This dual-edged transformation prompted critical reflection: despite the outward signs of technological splendor, had society truly come closer to achieving eudaimonia? Or had we embarked on a struggle where the achievements of modern science and industry remained fundamentally disconnected from, or even counteracted, true human flourishing? The tightly regimented factories of the Industrial Age not only reconfigured economies but also fundamentally altered the tapestry of everyday human existence. Here, in these sprawling epicenters of production, individuals were forced to adapt to systems that prized mechanical efficiency over creative spirit or personal satisfaction, creating a tension between economic progress and the delicate balance of overall human well-being that persists even in contemporary debates.

The complexity of our progress deepened further in the 20th century, an era marked by staggering global upheavals, transformative wars, and a rapidly globalizing economy. Here, the meaning of leadership expanded yet again, incorporating layers of geopolitical strategy, mass mobilization, and corporate innovation. The figure of the leader became multifaceted: no longer confined to the realms of tradition-bound statesmen or rugged industrial magnates, leaders now found themselves confronting the challenges of an interconnected world marked by rapid information exchange and cultural convergence. Outstanding figures such as Winston Churchill and Franklin D. Roosevelt each embodied distinct styles of leadership, merging personal ambition with the greater responsibilities demanded by their times. Meanwhile, corporate titans emerged as new forms of leaders - strategists who navigated the tumultuous waters of a global market and redefined the interplay between state and economy. Although their motivations ranged from the zeal of innovation to the pursuit of power and economic dominance, these leaders invariably confronted the fundamental challenge of aligning their personal ambitions with the broader, sometimes nebulous, needs and aspirations of the people they were entrusted to lead.

Today, as we find ourselves standing on the brink of yet another monumental transformation, the central axis of progress appears to revolve around data, automation, and the burgeoning realm of artificial intelligence. In this modern era, leadership has taken on a digital veneer. The contemporary champions of progress are not merely emperors or industrialists but are, instead, architects of virtual realities and stewards of a limitless technological frontier that continues to expand at a bewildering pace. With each new digital leap, we find ourselves grappling with profound ethical dilemmas: debates on the governance of AI - as exemplified by legislative measures like the EU's AI Act - serve as modern battlegrounds where the implications of unchecked technological advancements are fiercely contested. In this evolving landscape, the major question remains: Can current and future leaders balance the dizzying pace of innovation with the enduring necessity of safeguarding humanity's long-term interests? Is it possible for those who stand at the helm of technological revolutions to resist the irresistible allure of short-term gains in favor of policies and actions that nurture a future defined by sustained human flourishing?

The answer to these dilemmas is deeply rooted in an unwavering commitment to principled leadership. The historical record is replete with examples where leadership has risen to meet such challenges, even if not always with perfect outcomes. Consider, for instance, the legendary Antarctic expedition led by Sir Ernest Shackleton - a journey that might have been dismissed as a failure in its original objective of reaching a geographical end-point. Yet, Shackleton's expedition has come to symbolise an enduring lesson in leadership. His true measure was not in achieving the initial goal but in the extraordinary care and determination he demonstrated in ensuring the survival and well-being of his crew in the face of overwhelming odds. In those bitter, frigid expanses of the

Antarctic, where every decision teetered between hope and despair, Shackleton's legacy was forged not in conquest but through the profound capacity to inspire loyalty, to maintain morale, and to lead his men home safely when hope seemed all but lost. His story resonates across the ages as a timeless reminder that leadership is ultimately measured not by the acquisition of power, but by the responsibility one bears in nurturing the human spirit under the most adverse conditions.

As we gaze into the future, the challenges confronting our global society loom large and multifaceted. The relentless advance of climate change stands as one of the greatest existential threats of our time – an issue requiring long-term vision and the courage to make decisions not for fleeting political gain, but for the enduring benefit of future generations. The climate crisis calls for a form of leadership that is unburdened by the constraints of short-term electoral cycles and immediate gratification, but that is instead deeply committed to the stewardship of the planet over the coming century. It is a call for leaders who see the value in gradually transitioning away from fossil fuels towards a sustainable energy future, who understand that the survival of entire communities may depend on their willingness to reimagine established economic models. In the realm of corporate governance, too, leaders are increasingly confronted with critical dilemmas: how to balance the insatiable demand for shareholder value with the equally compelling need for long-term sustainability and social responsibility. As global capitalism continues to evolve, the very foundations upon which we base our economic systems are being interrogated – leading to debates over whether businesses may truly thrive if they operate with a regard for both profit and the broader public good. Philosophers like

Aristotle, whose teachings continue to provoke questions about the deeper purpose of human effort, would undoubtedly urge modern leaders to look beyond superficial benchmarks of success towards a vision that embraces the true essence of human flourishing.

In reflecting on these vast transformations, it becomes clear that leadership in every era has always been about more than merely wielding power. It is fundamentally about responsibility - about making choices that align immediate actions with a greater, long-term vision for the well-being of society at large. For each phase of our historical journey, whether marked by the enchanting promise of early human discovery, the structured innovations of ancient civilisations, the rebellious fervor of the Renaissance, or the robust industrial and digital transformations that continue today, the core principle remains the same: true progress is achieved when visionary leadership is coupled with ethical intent. Leaders must not only propel society forward in the name of innovation but must do so with an awareness of the far-reaching implications of their decisions. They must see beyond the transient allure of power and profit to embrace a model of leadership that is committed to the comprehensive, holistic thriving of humanity.

The story of human progress is inherently non-linear - it surges forward when propelled by firm convictions, recoils when missteps lead society astray, and then gathers momentum once more as new generations rise to the challenges of their time. Every epoch, with its victories and its setbacks, teaches us that leadership is not merely about ascending to positions of authority but about the continuous act of leading well. It is about instilling a lasting legacy of resilience, moral rectitude, and an unwavering commitment to the common good in the face of seemingly insurmountable obstacles.

In our current age, where technology, ethics, and governance are increasingly intertwined, leaders find themselves navigating a labyrinth of complicated dilemmas. The rapid advances in artificial intelligence, for instance, have opened up opportunities that were once confined to the realm of science fiction. Yet, these very innovations also raise profound ethical concerns. How can society ensure that these powerful tools remain in service to human aspirations rather than becoming instruments of control or oppression? When algorithms and data-driven decision-making begin to structure everyday life, it becomes essential for those at the helm to balance efficiency with empathy, and innovation with accountability. The debates surrounding the regulation of artificial intelligence, such as those encapsulated by the EU's AI Act, are not merely bureaucratic exercises; they reflect a broader philosophical struggle to manage change in a way that is consistent with recognized virtues and long-term societal well-being.

Let's also consider the transformative energies that have redefined our understanding of progress over the past several decades. The digital revolution, fueled by rapid advancements in communication, computing, and information technology, has dismantled traditional barriers of time and space. It has allowed for a democratisation of knowledge, enabling voices from every corner of the globe to partake in a once-unthinkable level of discourse and collaboration. Yet, with this revolution comes an equally significant responsibility - to ensure that the digital domain remains a space where human dignity and genuine dialogue can thrive, even as the very nature of leadership continues to evolve in the context of networks and virtual platforms. Today's digital architects are not merely custodians of technology; they are, in many ways, the modern torchbearers of progress, endlessly challenged to shape innovations that reflect a commitment to ethical responsibility and the nurturing of human potential.

The historical narrative of progress therefore becomes a rich tapestry, interwoven with threads of ambition, perseverance, and an enduring quest for excellence. It tells the story of countless leaders - visionaries who have reimagined the fabric of society, challenged established norms, and paved the way for future generations. From the embers of ancient campfires to the sophisticated circuits of modern digital systems, each chapter is imbued with a profound lesson: leadership is not a static set of characteristics, but an evolving practice that demands continual introspection, adaptation, and a relentless desire to serve the greater good.

Looking ahead, the challenges confronting our global society seem set to intensify. There is an urgency in addressing the existential threats posed by globalisation, digital misinformation, environmental degradation, and the potential for unrestrained technological disruption. In this context, the quality of leadership in the coming decades will serve as a litmus test for humanity's collective ability to adapt and flourish. It is incumbent upon current and future leaders to learn from the past - to draw wisdom from the perseverance of our forebears, the ingenuity of historical innovators, and the courage of those who have risked everything for the promise of a brighter tomorrow.

In the sphere of corporate governance, for instance, leaders must come to terms with the moral imperatives that now guide business practices. No longer can companies operate with a singular focus on short-term shareholder gains if they are to withstand the complex environmental and social challenges of our era. Modern corporate leadership demands a balanced approach, one that integrates sustainable practices with economic ambition, ensuring that every decision is weighed not just by its bottom-line impact, but by its contribution to societal well-being and environmental sustainability. The idea of capitalism is itself undergoing a rigorous reexamination - a process that calls upon leaders to redefine success in terms that are as much about ethical stewardship as they are about financial triumph.

The lessons of the past repeatedly remind us that the future of progress lies in the ability to lead with both wisdom and compassion. Whether it is the visionary pondering of ancient philosophers like Aristotle or the steadfast leadership of innovators who have transformed society, the underlying message resonates with clarity: leadership is fundamentally about guiding humanity toward a state where every individual has the opportunity to achieve true "flourishing". It is about building bridges across generational divides, fostering environments where innovation can coexist with ethical responsibility, and ensuring that every step taken in the march of progress is tempered by a deep commitment to the common good.

As we navigate an era marked by rapid technological change and unforeseen global challenges, it becomes apparent that the qualities needed in today's leaders are both familiar and revolutionary. Integrity above all else, they must also be, as always, courageous and visionary, yet they must also be attuned to the subtleties of social and ecological dynamics. The responsibilities they carry are immense, ranging from the intricate governance of artificial intelligence and digital networks to the broader stewardship of our shared environment and the well-being of future generations. This multifaceted role demands not only technical expertise and strategic acumen but also an abiding sense of moral duty - a recognition that every decision has the potential to shape the contours of human society for years to come.

In reflecting upon these themes, one cannot help but be reminded of the vast potential that lies in the union of purpose and progress. The next great chapters of our collective story will be written by those individuals who embrace this dual mandate - to lead not merely for the sake of leadership, but to champion a vision where progress is measured by the capacity of society to nurture its own humanity. Whether through groundbreaking innovations that revolutionize our daily lives or through policies that galvanize ethical governance on a global scale, the future, much like the past, will be defined by leaders who dare to place human flourishing at the center of their endeavors.

This expansive journey through the epochs of our civilisation teaches us that progress is neither inevitable nor guaranteed. It is, instead, the fruit of conscious choices made by individuals who understand the transformative power of leadership. From the rudimentary fires that first illuminated humanity's primal nights to the sophisticated digital networks that currently bind the world's information together, every advancement has been a testament to our species' enduring desire to reach beyond the known, to challenge the status quo, and to craft a legacy that future generations might inherit with pride and hope.

In conclusion, the very fabric of human advancement is woven with the threads of courageous decision-making and visionary leadership. The lessons derived from our past - each innovation, every social rearrangement, all the sweeping historical reforms - serve as both a guide and a clarion call for those who now find themselves at the helm of transformation. Leadership, in its most transcendent form, is not about amassing power for personal gain; it is about harnessing that power to serve a higher purpose. It is about building institutions, policies, and technologies that prioritise the well-being of all people and the sustainability of our planet.

As we stand on the brink of what many see as the next great revolution - an era dominated by digital innovation, automated systems, and artificial intelligence - the responsibility resting upon our shoulders is monumental. The debates on AI governance remind us that technological progress, while capable of producing unprecedented benefits, must be steered by ethical hands. The challenges of climate change, persisting social inequalities, and the complexities of modern corporate governance further underscore that our journey forward is not purely one of technological upgrade, but of deep ethical and political renewal. Only by integrating wisdom, compassion, and long-term vision into the practice of leadership can we hope to guide the flux of progress towards a future where every human being has the opportunity to flourish.

In the end, progress will remain forever bound to the quality of leadership that we choose to cultivate. True leaders must be both architects and custodians of a future that honors the lessons of the past while embracing the boundless possibilities of tomorrow. They must be willing to navigate the turbulent interplay between innovation and morality, to confront challenges head-on with both determination and empathy. And as we continue to chart the course of human history, it is this commitment to leading well that will ultimately determine whether our advances in science, technology, and social organization can indeed translate into a deeper, more enduring realization of human potential.

Thus, as we turn the page to the forthcoming chapters that will delve into the critical intersections of energy transitions, corporate strategy, and technological revolutions, let us hold fast to the understanding that leadership is not merely an exercise in authority – it is a profound act of responsibility. In every epoch, the quest for true progress has been intimately linked with the ability to lead with integrity, to forge paths that harmonise human ambition with ethical imperatives, and to inspire each generation to define success in terms of collective flourishing rather than isolated triumph. With each new breakthrough, whether borne of scientific inquiry or visionary policy, the enduring truth remains: that leadership is most noble when it is devoted to the service of all humanity, ensuring that every advance in the annals of history contributes not only to the expansion of our capabilities but also to the enrichment of our shared human experience.

In sum, the vast tableau of human history is a living testament to the fact that progress is an evolving, often tumultuous journey – marked by highs and lows, triumphs and setbacks – each chapter written by leaders who dared to dream and act upon their visions. Today, as tomorrow beckons with promises and perils alike, the call to lead with both vision and vigilance has never been more urgent. The leaders of our time and the generations yet to come will have to grapple with challenges and complexities that are as daunting as they are dynamic. Yet, it is precisely within this crucible of uncertainty and innovation that the true spirit of leadership can be most profoundly expressed – by transcending the limitations of the present and lighting the way towards a future defined by holistic, sustainable progress.

Let this be our guiding principle as we move forward: leadership is not merely about achieving goals through force or strategy, but about cultivating a culture of responsibility that honors the inherent dignity of every human being. It is about ensuring that our technological advances and economic endeavors serve to enhance, rather than diminish, the quality of life for all. It is about crafting a legacy that future generations will look back upon with admiration, not for the fleeting glories of transient victories, but for the enduring commitment to a vision where progress is truly synonymous with human flourishing.

Indeed, as we navigate the integrative domains of climate change, digital ethics, and global market transformations, the role of leadership emerges as the indispensable linchpin that binds these disparate realms together. It is the visionary leader who recognizes that innovation must be accompanied by empathy, that economic growth must be underpinned by social justice, and that technological progress must always align with the broader aspirations of a healthy, sustainable society. In embracing these ideals, we affirm that progress is not only a measure of what we achieve, but also a reflection of how we choose to achieve it.

Ultimately, the essence of leadership lies in the courage to guide, the wisdom to deliberate, and the integrity to act in ways that nurture the potential within each human soul. As we face the uncertainties of a rapidly changing world, let us commit to a form of leadership that transcends traditional metrics of success - one that is firmly anchored in the pursuit of an equitable, resilient, and humane future. This is the path that has always defined true progress, and it is the path that will continue to light our way in the face of tomorrow's challenges.

In closing, as we embark on the next phase of our collective, we must remember that the heart of progress beats in tandem with the principles of ethical leadership. The narrative of our past, from ancient fireside wisdom to the modern digital revolution, is a mirror reflecting our highest aspirations and our deepest challenges. It calls upon us to lead not merely with the power of innovation, but with the profound responsibility of ensuring that every step we take is a step towards a future where everyone has the chance to thrive.

This, then, is the enduring legacy of leadership: the unwavering commitment to not only advancing our physical and technological capabilities but also enriching the very soul of our civilisation. As we chart our course forward, we should do so with the clear understanding that the true measure of progress lies not in the towering heights of our achievements, but in the depth of our compassion, in the clarity of our vision, and in our unyielding dedication to creating a better, more just world for all.

For in every era – from the luminous glow of prehistoric fires to the dazzling screens of the digital age – the story of progress has been, and always will be, a story of leadership that dares to dream, unites disparate voices, and ultimately, leads humanity toward its highest potential.

2

Decision by Convergence

In the tumultuous arena of human endeavour, the ability to make decisions in an ever-changing landscape has always been a hallmark of great leadership. Decisions that stand the test of time are not simply matters of chance or the smooth execution of predetermined plans; they emerge from the persistent efforts of individuals and communities to harness a myriad of voices and experiences into a single, clear vision. This art of decision by convergence – where varied, sometimes conflicting perspectives merge to create a coherent path forward – has underpinned some of the most pivotal moments in human history. In this extended exploration, we will delve deep into the origins of this model, examine its applications from ancient democracies to contemporary corporate boardrooms, and then expand our focus to include a substantial discussion on strategy: from historic tactics and philosophies to modern-day approaches that are intricately connected with the significant global shift in energy transitions.

Long before the rise of modern corporations and the explosion of global technology reshaped our world, leaders, philosophers, and citizens alike were tasked with navigating crises and seizing opportunities through a process that transcended the mere pursuit of consensus. In ancient Athens, for instance, the Agora – a bustling centre of public discourse – was not just a market place but a crucible for ideas where philosophers and statesmen debated questions of state, virtue, and living. Here, voices clashed powerfully in a manner that is both invigorating and revealing; disagreements and passionate debates were not signs of factionalism but stepping stones toward a more inclusive democratic process.

In these lively exchanges, the process of convergence was evident; although no single citizen or philosopher had the absolute answer, the collective wisdom of those engaged in debate would eventually crystallise into policies and principles that laid the cornerstone of Western civilisation. Aristotle, whose philosophical tenets still resonate today, taught that the highest goal of human life is to achieve eudaimonia – a state of flourishing borne out of living in accordance with virtue and reason. In his view, true progress was not predicated on unanimous agreement at every turn but rather on a courageous mingling of divergent viewpoints that, when synthesised, could guide both individuals and communities towards a more vibrant, thriving existence.

The very notion of a flourishing society, as envisaged by Aristotle, depended on the collective effort to integrate various ideas into actionable wisdom. Whether it was reflecting on justice, ethics, or the role of the citizen, the process could only be achieved when differences, instead of fracturing the polis, were embraced as sources of insight. This ancient wisdom reminds us that the quest for progress is invariably tied to the capacity to welcome dissent as a vital ingredient in decision-making. It reveals that the art of convergence is as much about artfully blending competing perspectives as it is about the disciplined pursuit of a common good.

Fast forward several millennia, and the landscape has morphed into one dominated by boardrooms, parliaments, high-tech laboratories, and global communication networks. Despite the outwardly different settings, the underlying challenge remains unchanged: leaders today are inundated with an unending torrent of information, often arriving from multiple, sometimes contradictory sources. The pressure to reach a swift consensus in such an environment can have a paralysing effect. The phenomenon of groupthink – wherein the desire for uniformity suppresses dissent – is a constant danger. History has provided striking examples of where groupthink, rather than robust debate, led to cataclysmic outcomes.

The Bay of Pigs invasion is one such grim reminder. In this case, decision-makers became seduced by their own entrenched ideas, disregarding critical dissenting opinions and warning signs that could have altered an ill-conceived military plan. Even when has been voiced from within by some who foresaw the perils inherent in the plan, the drive towards uniformity blinded the group to the need for re-examination. Later, the Challenger Space Shuttle disaster would echo this same cautionary narrative. Engineers and experts had raised alarms about the integrity of the O-ring seals in the booster rockets; yet, in a bid to adhere to a rigid schedule and avoid dissent, these warnings fell on deaf ears. In this tragedy, the cost of neglecting diverse perspectives was unambiguously matched by the loss of both technology and life.

Such examples serve as potent illustrations of how the elusive balance between unity and diversity can either propel an organisation forward or cause it to crumble under the weight of its own internal pressures. It is clear that, while a forced consensus might seem efficient, it is the process of convergence – which embraces robust debate and disciplined synthesis – that allows a group to adapt and innovate with agility.

True leadership in today's intricate global theatre isn't about imposing one's will or dictating a singular viewpoint; it is about creating an environment that nurtures honest dialogue. It recognises that every dissenting voice may hold a shard of truth that, when combined with others, can illuminate the best path forward. Reed Hastings' adage of "farming for dissent" encapsulates this idea beautifully. In organisations where leadership actively encourages challenges to the status quo, innovation is not stifled but, rather, is allowed to unfurl organically. The healthiest organisations are those where team members are not afraid to articulate contrarian opinions, knowing that these contributions will eventually be distilled into a robust, well-rounded strategy.

For instance, consider a scenario in a modern technology firm that faces a critical strategic crossroad: whether to invest in an emerging, high-potential technology that also carries considerable risk. Opinions within the company might diverge sharply. Some voices might urge bold investment in the belief that innovation could deliver unprecedented returns, while others might caution that the risks could outweigh immediate benefits, advocating instead a focus on what the company already does well. In an environment driven solely by consensus, the resultant decision could become a watered-down compromise lacking the bold vision necessary to seize the opportunity. Alternatively, a convergence-based approach would begin with an active solicitation of diverse perspectives. Over time, through meaningful dialogue and pointed critical analysis, team members would start to see common threads in their disparate viewpoints, potentially recognising that although opinions on risk differ, there is a universally held belief in the transformative potential of the technology. The leader's role in this process is to craft a strategy that is inclusive and dynamic – one that artfully melds a calculated risk with measured pilot projects and comprehensive monitoring. In so doing, convergence not only transforms internal conflict into a fertile ground for innovation but also fortifies the organisation against unforeseen challenges.

Nowhere is the interplay between diverse perspectives and unified strategy more clearly illustrated than in the realm of strategic thought itself. Throughout history, strategy has evolved from rudimentary methods of warfare to the complex, multifaceted approaches seen in both business and governance today. Understanding the evolution of strategic thinking is crucial to grasping how convergence in decision-making has matured alongside our civilisation.

Ancient strategic wisdom can be seen in the teachings of Sun Tzu, whose seminal work, The Art of War, emphasised the importance of adaptability, deception, and the calculated integration of different tactical elements to outwit an opponent. Sun Tzu's insights were as much about understanding the enemy as they were about understanding oneself – a dual recognition of strengths and vulnerabilities. His strategies underscored the crucial need to incorporate a spectrum of intelligence and to question conventional wisdom when circumstances demanded a fresh perspective.

Similarly, the military tactics of ancient Roman legions were founded on a confluence of discipline, innovation, and the ability to harness diverse operational insights. Roman generals were renowned for their capacity to synthesise battlefield intelligence from scouts, engineers, and seasoned veterans into cohesive strategies that could adapt to ever-changing conditions. From these historic confluences emerged a paradigm of strategic leadership that prized the fusion of varied opinions into a singular, agile plan of action.

In the modern context, strategy has further evolved in response to the unprecedented challenges and opportunities posed by globalisation and technological disruptions. Contemporary strategists draw inspiration from historical precedents while simultaneously integrating cutting-edge developments in economics, data analytics, and behavioural science. Take, for example, the response to the global financial crisis of 2008. Many organisations found themselves bereft of clear direction, held captive by uncertain economic winds and outdated models. Yet, a smaller cohort of companies – those that had cultivated a culture of convergence – weathered the storm by gathering a diverse array of insights from experts in economics, risk management, and operations. Rather than clinging doggedly to a single strategy, these organisations adapted and pivoted, utilising the collective intelligence of diverse teams in real time. Their successes were a testament to the enduring value of convergence-based leadership: a model of decision-making that is neither static nor reliant on homogeneous thought, but rather one that prizes fluidity and adaptability.

The evolution of strategy from ancient approaches to contemporary methodologies has profoundly influenced how modern leaders approach decision-making. Today, the ability to integrate a wide range of perspectives into an effective strategy is seen as a competitive advantage in the relentless pursuit of innovation and progress. Organisations are no longer governed solely by the dictates of hierarchy or the prevailing winds of external opinion; they are instead led by visionaries who understand that sustainable growth and breakthrough ideas emerge when dissent and diversity are woven into the very fabric of organisational culture.

A significant contemporary application of this model can be found in the sphere of energy transitions – a subject that has commanded global attention in recent decades. The shift from traditional, fossil-fuel-centric energy models to renewable and sustainable alternatives is perhaps one of the most transformative changes in the recent history of human civilisation. This transition is emblematic of the convergence model of decision-making, where a multitude of disciplines – from technology and economics to environmental science and policy-making – must be integrated to form a coherent, forward-looking strategy.

The journey of energy transition illustrates the complexity and interconnectivity that are at the heart of the convergence process. Decades ago, energy production was largely focused on fossil fuels, guided by engineers and economists who worked within a well-established paradigm. However, as environmental concerns grew and the implications of climate change became undeniable, a chorus of new voices emerged. Scientists, environmental activists, policy experts, and technical innovators began to challenge the old models, advocating for a complete rethinking of how energy should be produced, distributed, and consumed.

In today's global landscape, the leadership required to steer this transition cannot rely on conventional, consensus-driven approaches. Instead, leaders must embrace the convergence of ideas that spans historical wisdom, contemporary analyses, and future projections. By actively soliciting opinions from diverse sectors – ranging from climate scientists warning of escalating global temperatures to brilliant engineers devising new renewable solutions – decision-makers can craft strategies that are both innovative and responsible. This convergence of expertise is akin to the ancient processes employed in the Agora of Athens, yet it operates on a global scale, addressing challenges that affect every corner of our interconnected world.

For instance, in the early stages of the energy transition, multinational corporations, governments, and research institutions forged what could be described as multidisciplinary teams. These teams blended the rigour of scientific inquiry with the pragmatism of economic forecasts and the visionary aspirations of environmental activists. The result was not a monolithic strategy but a dynamic blueprint that could evolve as new data emerged and as technological advancements continued apace. The principles of convergence that guided the dynamic debates in ancient societies became essential ingredients in these modern deliberations, ensuring that the path chosen was both resilient and adaptive.

Moreover, the strategic leadership that has emerged in the arena of energy transitions mirrors many of the lessons taught by historical figures such as Aristotle and Sun Tzu. It requires a deep commitment to achieving eudaimonia – a state of societal flourishing – by balancing economic growth with the imperative of environmental sustainability. Leaders today must navigate the complexities of market forces and technological innovation, all while fostering a culture where every stakeholder's voice is heard. This is not a mission for the faint-hearted; it is an ambitious pursuit that demands not only intellectual rigour but also compassion, foresight, and the courage to question established norms.

As we look at the global landscape, it becomes evident that the leaders who succeed in steering societies through these turbulent times are those who welcome the challenges of change. They recognise that the evolution towards renewable energy is not merely a technical adjustment but a profound shift in how humanity perceives its relationship with the natural world. This transition is a convergence of technology, policy reform, economic reorientation, and cultural evolution – a rich tapestry where every thread counts. Just as the integration of diverse philosophical and political ideas once laid the foundations of democracy in ancient Athens, today's leaders must integrate a kaleidoscope of insights to construct a sustainable future for all.

In the corporate realm, the very nature of strategy has undergone a metamorphosis in response to the volatility and uncertainty of our times. Contemporary business leaders are increasingly aware that the convergence of diverse ideas is not only a safeguard against the peril of groupthink but also a catalyst for radical innovation. From startups to multinational conglomerates, the process of decision-making now involves a deliberate effort to collect insights from a wide array of sources, engaging an assortment of internal experts and external advisors alike.

This evolution in leadership is evident in the emergence of multidisciplinary teams that bridge traditional silos. Modern strategy is no longer confined by rigid boundaries; it embraces a holistic view that accounts for environmental sustainability, technological innovation, market dynamics, and sociopolitical implications. For instance, many organisations today have established cross-functional innovation hubs, where experts from engineering, marketing, finance, and even sociology come together to craft strategies that are as versatile as they are forward-looking. This approach mirrors the convergence seen in historical forums, where only by bringing every perspective into the discussion could the group hope to forge a robust plan of action.

One particularly telling example can be traced to the evolution of digital strategy within industries that traditionally operated on older paradigms. These companies, facing the dual threats of disruption and obsolescence, turned to convergence-driven strategies to reinvent themselves. Rather than simply deploying digital technologies as an add-on to existing models, these forward-thinking leaders integrated digital transformation into the very core of their strategic planning processes. They recognised that this integration required open dialogue, an acceptance of dissenting opinions, and a willingness to re-evaluate long-held assumptions. In doing so, they not only navigated turbulent market conditions but also positioned themselves at the vanguard of a digital revolution that continues to reshape global commerce.

Another contemporary illustration of convergence in strategy is the agile response to crises such as the global financial downturn and the more recent disruptions caused by geopolitical tensions and climate-related events. Organisations that had embedded a culture of active dissent and robust debate found themselves better prepared to pivot their strategies when uncertainty loomed large. These organisations did not simply wait for external forces to shape their destiny; they proactively sought out diverse perspectives, debated their implications, and then synthesised these insights into highly adaptive operational models. This capacity to pivot, adjust course, and innovate under pressure is the very hallmark of convergence-based leadership and one of its most valuable assets in an era marked by rapid change.

Indeed, the evolution of strategic thinking from historical to contemporary contexts reflects a broader transformation in our understanding of leadership. In the past, the focus was often on hierarchical decision-making, where power and authority were concentrated in the hands of a few. Today, leadership is fundamentally about collaboration; it is about creating networks of ideas that span across disciplines, industries, and even national boundaries. The leaders of tomorrow will be those who not only harness the wisdom of diverse viewpoints but also actively seek out dissent, knowing that the friction of debate is what polishes raw ideas into strategies of lasting impact.

The interplay between convergent decision-making and strategic leadership becomes even more apparent when we consider the monumental global endeavour of energy transitions. The shift from a fossil-fuel economy to one anchored by renewable energy is one of the most comprehensive challenges we have ever faced. It requires not only technological innovation but also a fundamental rethinking of economic, social, and environmental paradigms. In many ways, the energy transition is a test case in modern convergence – a scenario where every stakeholder, from government officials and industry leaders to local communities and environmental activists, must engage in a process of collective decision-making.

Drawing on the lessons of both historical strategy and contemporary strategic innovations, leaders in the field of energy transitions are tasked with navigating a delicate balance between ambition, caution, and accountability. They must be adept at synthesising a broad array of insights – from the latest scientific research on climate change to emerging market trends in renewable energy technologies – and then converting these insights into operational strategies that are both bold and pragmatic. For example, leading energy firms today are investing in pilot projects and rigorous testing phases that allow them to explore new technologies without committing fully to unproven concepts. This measured approach ensures that risks are mitigated while still enabling the organisation to seize opportunities for innovation.

Furthermore, the convergence paradigm extends beyond the technical and economic challenges to include social and cultural dimensions. As communities across the globe increasingly demand sustainability and environmental justice, the voices of local residents, indigenous groups, and community activists must be woven into the fabric of national and international energy policies. This inclusive approach, which mirrors the ancient debates of the Athenian Agora, helps to ensure that strategies are not only economically viable but also ethically sound and socially responsive. In this way, convergence-based leadership in energy transitions becomes a powerful instrument for societal transformation, one that integrates the legacies of historical strategic thought with the imperatives of modern sustainability.

The Role of Humility and Courage in Convergent Leadership

At the heart of successful convergence in both decision-making and strategic planning is an ethos of humility and courage. Leaders must be willing to acknowledge the limits of their own expertise and open themselves to the rich, often challenging, insights of others. This willingness to admit that one's own perspective may be incomplete is the first step towards creating an environment where dissent is viewed not as a threat but as a valuable resource. It takes courage to challenge established assumptions and to pivot away from a path that may have once seemed secure. Yet, it is this very courage that underpins the capacity to transform conflict into constructive dialogue and, ultimately, into innovative action.

History is replete with examples where a lack of such humility led to disastrous outcomes. The Challenger Space Shuttle disaster serves as a stark illustration of what can happen when dissenting voices are suppressed in favour of maintaining a façade of unanimity. In that instance, the prevailing culture of conformity within NASA led to the tragic sidelining of engineers who raised legitimate concerns about the integrity of critical components. Conversely, the success of the Apollo missions provides a powerful counter-narrative. Here, a culture of open debate, inclusive of diverse perspectives and even outright challenges to conventional wisdom, paved the way for one of humanity's most extraordinary achievements. The ability to integrate myriad viewpoints under rigorous scrutiny ultimately allowed NASA to mitigate risks and innovate in the face of seemingly insurmountable challenges.

In today's fast-paced global environment, the importance of cultivating such a culture cannot be overstated. Leaders who invest in fostering an atmosphere of constructive dissent – where every voice, regardless of its source, is heard and valued – create organisations that are resilient, adaptable, and poised for breakthrough innovation. It is through this delicate interplay of humility and courage that convergence-based decision-making becomes a potent strategy for navigating the complexities of modern challenges, be they in corporate boardrooms, political arenas, or the transformative arena of energy transitions.

Reflecting on these themes, one cannot help but return to the wisdom of Aristotle, whose enduring teachings continue to illuminate our path forward. His vision of achieving eudaimonia – a state of flourishing that is attainable through the balanced integration of reason, virtue, and collective intelligence – remains as relevant today as it was in ancient times. Aristotle believed that virtue lies in finding the mean between extremes, a principle that resonates deeply with the challenges of modern decision-making. In our contemporary context, the pursuit of the best possible outcome in uncertain times is not about eliminating conflict but rather about harnessing it as fuel for innovation and progress.

The modern leader is thus called not to be an authoritarian figure dictating the course of action from atop a pedestal, but rather a facilitator of a grand dialogue. They must create spaces where critical questions are posed without fear of reprisal and where every voice can contribute its unique insight to the unfolding narrative of progress. This is a leadership style that requires both the analytical rigour of an ancient philosopher and the agile, adaptive mindset of a modern strategist. It is a balance that, when struck, not only propels organisations forward but also underscores the broader human pursuit of a society in which every individual – and every idea – is valued.

As we stand on the threshold of unprecedented challenges – from the relentless pace of technological change and global market disruptions to the existential threats posed by climate change – the call for convergence has never been more urgent. The leaders of tomorrow will be defined by their ability to counter conventional wisdom, to welcome dissent as essential, and to synthesise a dazzling array of perspectives into strategies that are as resilient as they are visionary. Their success will be measured not merely in economic or technological terms but in the enduring impact they have on the quality of life and the sustainable well-being of communities across the globe.

A glimpse into the future reveals that this is not a journey of simple linear progress. Rather, it is an ongoing process of reflection, debate, adaptation, and renewal. As history has shown us, breakthroughs often emerge from periods of intense challenge and even apparent chaos. It is in these moments that the process of convergence – the artful integration of diverse ideas – becomes crucial. When leaders are prepared to champion the multiplicity of voices that comprise a vibrant and innovative community, they create the conditions for a future in which every challenge is met with a well-considered, multi-dimensional response.

At its core, the philosophy of convergence in decision-making is a celebration of diversity in all its forms. It recognises that the varied experiences, insights, and skills of individuals are not obstacles to be tamed but assets to be harnessed. In every field – from politics and business to science and technology – the collective wisdom of a diverse community is the linchpin of progress. Leaders who see beyond the confines of their own perspective and actively seek to incorporate a broad tapestry of voices are the ones who will shape a future that honours our past while boldly confronting the challenges of tomorrow.

This inclusive approach is especially critical when we contemplate the scale and complexity of global energy transitions. The movement towards renewable energy sources is fundamentally an exercise in convergence. It is not enough to invest solely in technological innovation or policy reform; the transformation must be driven by an integrated strategy that recognises the interconnectedness of environmental sustainability, economic viability, and social equity. In this endeavour, the lessons of history are poignantly relevant. Just as the deliberations in the ancient Athenian Agora laid the groundwork for democracy, so too does the process of convergence underpin the strategic efforts to build a sustainable energy future.

What does a convergence-based energy strategy look like in practice? It begins by inviting experts from across the spectrum – engineers developing next-generation solar panels, economists modelling the long-term impacts of renewable investments, sociologists examining the broader societal implications of a green economy, and policymakers crafting the regulatory frameworks needed to support these initiatives. These diverse insights are then brought together in forums that value both rigorous debate and the collaborative synthesis of ideas. Pilot projects, scenario planning, and iterative feedback loops are employed to refine the strategies, ensuring that risks are managed while innovation continues unabated.

This model of strategic convergence is not merely about immediate problem-solving; it is about laying the foundations for a future where progress is measured not solely by short-term metrics but by the sustained impact on human flourishing. Leaders who embrace this approach understand that the ultimate goal is to secure a future where economic growth, technological innovation, and environmental stewardship are seamlessly integrated into the fabric of society - a future where our energy systems are both resilient and regenerative.

As we draw together this extensive exploration of convergence, strategy, and energy transitions, one theme emerges with clarity: the journey towards effective decision-making is as much about the internal culture of an organisation as it is about its external strategies. The willingness to challenge established norms, to welcome dissenting opinions, and to synthesise these myriad inputs into a coherent vision is the essence of true leadership. It requires not only intellectual flexibility but also a profound commitment to the broader ideals of justice, sustainability, and human flourishing.

The challenges ahead are formidable. Whether it is addressing the multifaceted dimensions of climate change, navigating the dizzying pace of technological disruption, or realigning global economic systems to better serve the collective good, the task before us is both daunting and exhilarating. The convergence approach to decision-making provides a powerful tool for meeting these challenges head-on. It is through the fusion of diverse insights - drawn from the annals of ancient philosophy through the crucibles of modern strategy, and now seamlessly integrated into the pressing demands of energy transitions - that we can forge a path towards a world where every decision, however complex, becomes a stepping stone toward a brighter, more sustainable future.

In conclusion, the art of decision by convergence represents far more than a modern managerial technique; it is a timeless pursuit that has shaped the evolution of human civilisation. From the spirited debates of ancient Athens to the high-stakes strategic manoeuvres in contemporary boardrooms, the ability to meld disparate viewpoints into a coherent, visionary strategy has proven to be the secret sauce behind many of history's most transformative moments. As we embark on this new era - one defined by rapid technological change, global environmental challenges, and the urgent need for sustainable energy transitions - leaders who can harness the power of convergence will be best positioned to lead us towards a more innovative and inclusive future.

The lessons of the past, the dynamic insights of contemporary thinkers, and the pressing imperatives of our present converge to guide us towards the future. It is a future in which the integration of divergent ideas is not a luxury but a necessity; a future in which the art of decision-making demands the courage to challenge established paradigms, the humility to learn from every voice, and the strategic foresight to build a resilient, thriving society. As we move forward, let us carry these lessons close, recognising that every debate, every dissent, and every moment of convergence is a building block upon which our sustainable future is constructed.

The journey toward convergence is a testament to the enduring potential of collective wisdom and the transformative power of inclusive, adaptive leadership. It invites us all to reimagine what is possible when differences are celebrated rather than suppressed, and when every voice is given the chance to contribute to the ongoing dialogue of progress. In this convergence lies the promise not only of better decision-making, but of a better, more sustainable world - a world where economic innovation, social inclusivity, and environmental stewardship coexist and flourish in harmony.

As we stand at this pivotal moment, facing challenges that are as complex as they are urgent, the call for convergence is clearer than ever. The path ahead may be fraught with obstacles, but it is also illuminated by the promise of extraordinary human potential – the promise that when diverse minds come together under visionary leadership, the seemingly insurmountable can be transformed into the achievable. Let us therefore embrace the art of decision by convergence as both our guiding principle and our ongoing challenge – a challenge that, when met with determination, ingenuity, and empathy, can ultimately transform not just our organisations, but the very fabric of our civilisation.

In the annals of leadership history, we have seen empires rise and fall, innovations spark revolutions, and communities overcome adversity. The common thread through all these narratives is the capacity to listen, to learn, and to merge insights in pursuit of a common goal. Today, as we tackle issues that bridge the gap between energy transitions, economic justice, and global sustainability, the need for convergence-based decision-making is more than an abstract concept – it is a practical strategy that can guide us through tumultuous times and towards a future where every individual and every community can truly flourish.

Ultimately, the art of decision by convergence offers a roadmap for living a life of purpose, grounded in the knowledge that true progress is achieved not by silencing dissent, but by transforming it into a symphony of ideas that together create a vision more compelling than any single perspective could ever achieve. This is the timeless pursuit of coherent, visionary leadership – a pursuit that, when embraced wholeheartedly, promises to redefine our future in ways that honour our past, address the challenges of the present, and pave the way for a sustainable, enlightened tomorrow.

The narrative of human progress is, at its heart, a story of converging paths - a mosaic of voices, experiences, and strategies coming together to form the blueprint of a better world. As we continue to chart our collective destiny, let us draw upon the rich tapestry of historical wisdom, modern strategic insights, and the transformative potential of energy transitions to guide us. In so doing, we not only honour the legacy of those who came before us but also lay the foundation for a future defined by resilience, innovation, and the unwavering pursuit of human flourishing.

In closing, we can say that the journey of decision by convergence - from the lively debates of ancient forums to today's boundless technological and environmental challenges - is one of the most significant narratives in our evolutionary story. Its lessons, deeply rooted in history and powerfully relevant in the present, call upon each of us to participate actively in this ongoing dialogue. Only by doing so can we hope to build a future that is as rich in diversity and innovation as the ideas that forged it.

3

Innovation from Galileo to DARPA

Throughout the long and winding corridors of human progress, there has been one constant force that binds every era, every civilisation, and every spirit seeking to better itself - a force we call innovation. It is a force that has, time and again, broken through the barriers of tradition and convention to usher in transformative changes that have reshaped the very fabric of our existence. It is a narrative not merely of invention, but of the courage to challenge the status quo, a narrative whose chapters stretch from the ancient, introspective days of early Christianity through the bold astronomical assertions of Galileo, to the modern laboratories and tightly wound innovation networks of organisations such as DARPA. In this tale there emerges a continuous interplay between passion for discovery, respect for tradition, and the unmistakable imprint of visionary leadership that has guided these revolutionary endeavours.

In the early whispers of Christianity, when faith and doctrine intermingled with the mystique of revelation, there emerged a subtle yet powerful doctrine known as the Commonitorium.

It was in this milieu that the venerable Vincent de Lérins, a monk of the 5th century whose words echoed with the gravitas of a sage, became a principal voice guiding the spiritual and intellectual journey of his age. His famous injunction, "Avoid profane novelty; hold tightly to antiquity," was not a rejection of the new but a caution against abandoning the enduring wisdom that had been accrued over generations. In these hallowed discussions, innovation was viewed both with wonder and apprehension. The Commonitorium was the conscience of an era, reminding all that while the quest for the new was vital, it must never come at the cost of forsaking long-held truths that had provided a steady light through the darkness of uncertainty.

Yet, even as the echoes of Vincent's admonitions reverberated in the serene cloisters and echoing halls of early monasteries, the world outside was stirring with its own visions of progress. In the 17th century, a period of brilliant scientific discovery and contentious religious debates, Europe was gripped by the relentless quest for knowledge amidst the backdrop of maritime prowess and the insatiable need to conquer the uncharted territories of the seas. European powers such as Venice, the Netherlands, France, and Spain were not content with the mysteries of the horizon remaining unsolved. They decreed handsome prizes for those who could devise a method to determine longitude at sea - a challenge that promised not only to unlock the secrets of navigation but also to secure economic and political dominance.

Among the brave souls who answered this call were the likes of Christiaan Huygens and the indomitable Galileo Galilei. Galileo, whose name is now synonymous with the revolutionary pursuit of astronomical knowledge, dared to let his gaze stray beyond what was then considered the acceptable norm. With a mind that was as curious as it was ingenious, he proposed to harness the rhythmic dance of Jupiter's moons as a mechanism by which the longitude of a vessel might be determined. His idea, radical and audacious in equal measure, suggested that these celestial bodies could serve as a cosmic timepiece, their positions intricately recording the passage of time and space. In a spirit of unwavering conviction, Galileo ventured his proposal to Spain, speaking not only of the science of the heavens but also of the practical applications that could transform maritime ventures. The mechanical artefact born of his ideas – the Galilean calculator – now resides in the hallowed halls of Florence's Istituto e Museo di Storia della Scienza, standing as an enduring testament to his brilliance and his relentless commitment to progress.

Galileo's scientific endeavours, however, were as interwoven with his intellectual genius as they were with the shifting tides of politics and power. His work would not have flourished without the support and protection of the Medici family, whose influence in the courts of Italy offered him a rare shield against the often harsh censure of the Catholic Church. In an age when deviation from established doctrine carried with it the risk of not only condemnation but of dire personal peril, the Médicis' patronage was nothing short of revolutionary. Even as Galileo was forced to contend with ecclesiastical opposition – his assertions about heliocentrism viewed as heretical by many at the time – he persisted in his quest, driven by the belief that the pursuit of truth was an endeavour worth all sacrifices. Though he was unable to complete his design of an accurate longitudinal clock for the Dutch prize before his death, his vision outlived him. His son eventually brought his father's ideas to tangible fruition seven years later, and it was only centuries later, in 1992, that Pope John Paul II would formally acknowledge what Galileo had long maintained – that the Earth indeed revolves around the sun.

This voyage through the chapters of history reveals a fascinating interplay between the cautious defence of tradition and the unbridled daring of innovation. The struggle to balance these two opposing but complementary forces is one that stretches across centuries. As humankind has journeyed from the contemplative halls of early Christian monasticism to the bustling, experimental laboratories of the modern world, the tension between venerating the past and embracing the potential of the new has been a perennial theme. It is a dialectic that speaks to the essence of progress – the simultaneous need to respect the accumulated wisdom of antiquity, even as we push forward into uncharted territories of discovery.

Indeed, our journey through the annals of innovation would be incomplete without a nod to Niccolò Machiavelli, whose writings from the Renaissance period provide a kaleidoscopic view of change and the diverse types of leadership that influence innovation. Machiavelli's contemplations, as presented in his seminal works "The Prince" and "The Discourses," unravel a duality in the way innovation is conceived and enacted. In "The Prince," innovation is portrayed as a bold and sweeping endeavour, a fiery tempest that upends the established order of governance. One can vividly imagine a ruler standing at a critical crossroads, contemplating radical departures from tradition in order to reinvent the very mechanisms of power and authority. To such a prince, breaking free from the shackles of the past was not merely an option - it was an existential imperative. Innovation, in this context, is likened to a masterful brushstroke on the canvas of power, wielding change as if it were a sword capable of cutting through stagnant legacies and mediocrity. Machiavelli hints that, in the realm of statecraft, embracing change with all its inherent risks can lead to the forging of legacy; inaction, on the other hand, portends decay and vulnerability.

Yet, Machiavelli's discourse does not remain monolithic in its treatment of innovation. In "The Discourses," he adopts a contrasting perspective, one that reveals innovation as a journey back to the fundamentals of greatness. In this alternative vision, innovation is not always about radical reinvention but can be a process of rediscovery - of reaching back to the pristine ideals that once animated the best of our past. Much like a phoenix rising majestically from the ashes, this form of innovation seeks to cleanse what has become tarnished over time and restore the original purity of institutions and principles that have been diluted by the vagaries of human experience. The Renaissance thinker, with his ink-stained fingers and reflective prose, seemed to suggest that even as we pursue the future with fervour, there is wisdom in reclaiming and reinvigorating those enduring truths that have weathered the test of time.

It is therefore not surprising that innovators throughout history have been a study in paradox - a juxtaposition of audacity and conservatism, of risk-taking coupled with an abiding respect for accumulated knowledge. For many, the mantle of the innovator was not something that could be embraced lightly. Instead, innovation was often thrust upon individuals by the urgent demands of their epoch, a call that required them to dance on the precarious edge of possibility while contending with the ever-looming spectre of failure. Machiavelli's writings capture this delicate balance perfectly, a balance that remains relevant in every era, be it on the stages of Renaissance Italy or in the corporate boardrooms of the twenty-first century.

As the centuries turned and the industrial age dawned with its incandescent promise of progress, the narrative of innovation began to take on new dimensions. In 1934, an economist by the name of Joseph Schumpeter emerged with a groundbreaking conceptualisation of innovation that resonated deeply with the dynamism of a changing world. Schumpeter's observations, rich in both insight and practical implications, defined innovation as the creation of new combinations of the old and the new – an intermingling of knowledge, resources, technology, and ventures that breathed new life into old ideas. For Schumpeter, the act of innovation was not limited to the mere act of invention; it encompassed the entire process of transforming an idea into something that could be tangibly realised in the marketplace. He drew a clear distinction between invention, which represented the germination of an idea or a prototype, and innovation, which signified the process of nurturing that idea to fruition, thereby enabling it to generate value within a commercial context.

Schumpeter's revolutionary perspective liberated innovation from the narrow confines of purely academic thought, positioning it instead as the engine that powered capitalist entrepreneurship. In his view, the dynamism of an economy was not solely predicated on the appearance of novel gadgets or the sudden emergence of a groundbreaking product; rather, it lay in the relentless pursuit of new business models, the continuous reimagining of existing processes, and the indefatigable drive to solve practical problems with creative solutions. In the modern marketplace, this marriage of scientific discovery and commercial ambition has become the lifeblood of progress, ensuring that innovation remains not just a fleeting burst of brilliance, but a perennial force that drives economic growth and societal advancement.

As Schumpeter's ideas took root, the nature of innovation itself began to evolve further, branching out into new arenas of thought and practice. It became increasingly clear that innovation need not be the solitary pursuit of a lone genius huddled away in the darkness of a distant lab. Rather, it could be a collaborative enterprise - a coordinated dance of minds, combining efforts from within and beyond the confines of individual organisations. This understanding gave birth to the concept of open innovation, a model that would radically alter the way that companies and institutions approached problem-solving and development.

The notion of open innovation, as introduced by Professor Henry Chesbrough of Berkeley in 2003, underscores a modern approach to innovation that values the contributions of external sources as much as those of the internal R&D teams. Rather than confining creative energies to the insular walls of a single company, the open innovation paradigm spotlights the fact that groundbreaking ideas can emerge from unexpected quarters - a research institution, a start-up tucked away in an overlooked corner, or even an individual with sheer passion and ingenuity. The open model recognises that in a world as richly interconnected as ours, the best ideas are often the product of collaboration between disparate groups, each contributing a unique perspective and a different set of skills to the collective endeavour.

As business leaders began to appreciate this multifaceted approach to innovation, the distinctions between closed and open models became a subject of much debate. In organisations that adhered to the closed innovation philosophy, the process was one of rigorously controlled internal development, where teams worked in relative isolation from the wider world. In such settings, knowledge was treated as a guarded commodity, innovation was conceived as an internally brewed secret, and success was measured by the ability to keep breakthroughs hidden from competitors until they could be monetised. Apple, for instance, became synonymous with such a model during its formative years, developing its groundbreaking products behind veiled secrecy in an environment that eschewed external collaboration.

In contrast, an open innovation philosophy recognises that the best results can be achieved when knowledge is allowed to flow freely across institutional barriers. It is an approach that celebrates the idea that intellectual property, when shared judiciously and managed rightly, can become a catalyst for new discoveries and transformative breakthroughs. Companies embracing this collaborative model actively seek partnerships with external entities, pooling resources, expertise, and insights in order to drive innovation forward. In these arrangements, the process of innovation is more akin to a grand conversation – one in which each participant contributes to a shared vision of the future, and where the resulting innovations are the product of a collective rather than an individual endeavour.

Of course, this approach to collaboration is not without its challenges. It requires a radical shift in mindset - a willingness to venture beyond one's established comfort zone and to engage in a dialogue with other thinkers and doers. It also demands that organisations carefully weigh the benefits of sharing knowledge against the risks associated with relinquishing proprietary control. As researchers and practitioners in the field have noted, more openness is not always synonymous with better outcomes; the key lies in striking the delicate balance between collaboration and confidentiality, in recognising when to share and when to safeguard.

As the debate between open and closed innovation matured, it was evident that the solutions to some of the world's most intractable problems often lay not in isolated genius, but in the collective wisdom of many hands and minds coming together. This lesson was brought into sharp focus by the evolution of global challenges - complex, multifaceted issues that could scarcely be solved by any single entity or discipline alone. Whether in the realms of environmental sustainability, political reform, or the pursuit of breakthroughs in energy and technology, innovation has come to be seen as a process that is as much about forging partnerships as it is about individual creativity.

It is in this grand tapestry of ideas and innovations that one finds another remarkable chapter - a chapter that shines a light on the extraordinary accomplishments of an organisation that has consistently pushed the boundaries of what is possible: DARPA, the Defense Advanced Research Projects Agency. Born out of the urgency of the Cold War era and the shock of Sputnik's launch in 1957, DARPA was established with a singular mission - to ensure that the United States would never again be caught flat-footed by technological surprises from an adversary. In this spirit of urgency and boundless determination, DARPA quickly evolved into a curator of breakthrough science and a beacon of technical excellence.

The early days of DARPA were marked by a remarkable blend of patriotism, visionary leadership, and a profound belief in the transformative power of research. Its first director, Roy Johnson, epitomised the sense of mission that animated the agency. In 1958, Johnson famously left a lucrative post at General Electric to accept a much humbler salary at DARPA - a decision that underscored his commitment to national service and to the central belief that sometimes the most noble endeavours require sacrifices on a personal scale. Such dedication would come to define the agency, as DARPA embarked on a series of projects that would not only alter the trajectory of military technology but also fundamentally reshape the very contours of modern society.

One of DARPA's most legendary achievements was the creation of ARPANET in 1969, a project that would eventually sow the seeds from which the vast and pervasive network of the Internet would grow. Born out of the imperative to link disparate computer systems across geographically scattered research projects, ARPANET was a visionary experiment that sought to transform the way in which people and machines communicated. The project began modestly, connecting a handful of nodes located at premier institutions such as UCLA, UC Santa Barbara, the Stanford Research Institute, and the University of Utah. Yet, within a couple of years, ARPANET had evolved into a proof-of-concept that would pave the way for a revolution in global connectivity. By 1971, this fledgling network had achieved a level of operational functionality that hinted at the boundless potential of interlinked systems – a potential that would, over subsequent decades, completely reimagine the world of commerce, communication, and community.

But DARPA's impact was not confined solely to the realm of digital communication. Over the course of its storied history, the agency has been the orchestrator of some truly extraordinary technological leaps. With a nimble cadre of only 220 employees managing nearly 250 research programmes at any given moment, DARPA has mastered the art of rapid, focused innovation. Its approach was far removed from the bureaucratic inertia that often hampers large governmental bodies; instead, DARPA operated much like an elite special forces unit, striking swiftly and decisively at the heart of technological challenges. This agility and emphasis on daring, high-risk projects have allowed DARPA to spearhead innovations that have not only redefined military capabilities but have also spilled over into the civilian sphere, affecting everything from computing to satellite navigation.

One of the early projects undertaken by DARPA was MULTICS, or the Multiplexed Information and Computing Service, initiated in 1965 in collaboration with researchers at MIT. MULTICS was an ambitious programme aimed at creating a computing environment that would allow remote terminals to connect seamlessly, support a range of applications, and operate continuously across a network. Though the project itself did not yield a commercial product, the conceptual and technological foundations it established proved to be instrumental in the development of later operating systems such as Unix – a system that would go on to influence the entire field of computing, culminating in innovations that now underpin modern cloud computing. It is a fascinating irony that while DARPA did not directly invent what contemporary culture recognises as "the cloud," its early experiments with MULTICS sowed the seeds from which the cloud's transformative potential would eventually grow.

Elsewhere, DARPA's quest for technological supremacy also ushered in the precursor to what is now known as the Global Positioning System. In the wake of Sputnik's startling launch, U.S. physicists at the Johns Hopkins Applied Physics Laboratory discerned a method to exploit radio transmissions and the Doppler effect to lock onto the satellite's precise location. Through a brilliant reversal of this technology, they laid the groundwork for determining an observer's position relative to a satellite. This was the genesis of what would become a global navigation system, an invention that has intricately woven itself into the daily lives of millions around the world. The transformation of military innovation into a ubiquitous tool for civilian navigation is yet another stirring testament to the far-reaching consequences of embracing bold ideas.

A particularly imaginative endeavour from DARPA's storied past was the Aspen Movie Map project, executed in collaboration with MIT researchers around 1979. In an era long before the ubiquitous presence of digital mapping services, the Aspen Movie Map endeavoured to offer viewers a virtual tour of the snow-laden streets of Aspen, Colorado. Video cameras mounted on a moving vehicle captured a series of images that, when compiled in the correct order, offered a visual narrative of the city's layout. This early experiment in virtual reality and street-level mapping presaged the digital cartography solutions that today enable real-time navigation with unerring accuracy. In every instance where DARPA's projects have taken root, they have not only solved immediate tactical challenges but have also laid down the philosophical and practical blueprints for countless other innovations.

The journey from early Christian meditations on tradition to DARPA's audacious experiments on the frontiers of technology is a long arc of daring vision and steadfast purpose. At each juncture in this expansive narrative, leaders have risen who embody the essence of innovation. Whether it was the contemplative warnings of Vincent de Lérins - a reminder that not all novelty is beneficial - or the passionate defiance of Galileo and his contemporaries, these figures have demonstrated that progress is born out of a willingness to challenge and disrupt the norm.

In our modern era, characterised by rapid technological change and global interconnectivity, organisations find themselves facing challenges that mirror the complexities of history in both scale and depth. Corporate research budgets are no longer investments in isolated experiments; rather, they are strategic exercises aimed at preserving competitiveness in a relentlessly dynamic marketplace. In environments where most companies map out linear trajectories spanning three to five years or more, there exists an almost universal blueprint among industry leaders - many of whom have converged on similar visions of the future. In such an environment, truly transformative innovation requires more than incremental change; it necessitates a structured yet nimble approach to experimentation, one that recognises the critical importance of both scientific emergence and user-centred design.

Companies today must navigate a delicate web woven from abstract scientific insights and tangible, utilitarian needs. They engage in a form of strategic choreography, defining projects that simultaneously address the latest in scientific breakthroughs while meeting the evolving requirements of consumers and end-users. It is this dual focus that can empower organisations to remain not only relevant but also resilient in the face of shifting technological landscapes. The process is demanding, requiring strict time constraints and clearly articulated goals that instil a sense of urgency and purpose. A prime example of such a strategic vision can be seen in the ambitious efforts to develop hypersonic vehicles. Here, the objective was not merely to unravel the mysteries of high-speed aerodynamics but to harness that knowledge in the service of national security. Achievements such as achieving sustained aerodynamically controlled flight at speeds exceeding Mach 20 are emblematic of the way in which innovation can simultaneously serve strategic imperatives while advancing the frontiers of science.

In the evolving discourse on innovation, it is imperative to recognise that success does not occur in a vacuum but is the cumulative result of both internal vision and external collaboration. This realisation has propelled the rise of centres of innovation - vast, geographically concentrated hubs where academic institutions, corporate giants, and governmental agencies converge to address the so-called "wicked problems" of our time. These problems, whether they be environmental conundrums, political challenges, or the quest for sustainable energy solutions such as nuclear fusion, defy simple, isolated approaches. They demand enormous collaborative efforts, pooling resources and intellectual capital in a manner that no single organisation can achieve independently.

It is in these collaborative crucibles that the full spectrum of innovation - from the sparks of audacious ideas to the meticulous shaping of new technologies – finds its most fertile ground. The modern landscape is one where the geographic clustering of talent and resources is becoming increasingly significant. Future generations of scientists and engineers from prestigious institutions like Cornell, Caltech, Berkeley, and MIT are likely to gravitate towards these hubs, lured by the promise of working on projects that are borderless in their ambition and revolutionary in their potential. This convergence of talent and technology will not only redefine the way innovation is conducted but will also reinforce the crucial importance of leadership in navigating this rapidly changing environment.

As we reflect on the grand tapestry of human endeavour, it becomes evident that innovation has always been inextricably linked with leadership. Whether in the silent cloisters where ancient monks guarded timeless wisdom or in the bustling laboratories where scientists like Galileo challenged the heavens, leaders have consistently demonstrated that the courage to innovate is a fundamental element of effective governance. The lessons of history are unambiguous: true leadership involves the ability to both ignite the flames of revolution and to temper them with the steady hand of experience and prudence.

DARPA's story offers one of the most compelling examples of this dynamic. At its core, DARPA is not just a repository of brilliant engineers or cutting-edge research programmes – it is a testament to the transformative power of visionary leadership. The agency's unconventional methods, its capacity to operate with the decisiveness of a tactical unit rather than the inertia of a bureaucratic machine, and its relentless pursuit of breakthroughs have made it a beacon for organisations across the globe. DARPA's leadership did not come from a place of comfortable conformity; it emerged from an understanding that the only way to truly move forward is to embrace uncertainty, to confront the unknown with a blend of scientific rigour and creative audacity.

Through the lens of DARPA's initiatives - projects such as ARPANET, MULTICS, the precursor technologies to GPS, and even pioneering experiments in virtual mapping - we are reminded that innovation, in its most profound form, is about more than just technological progress. It is about creating a culture where risk is celebrated as a necessary counterpart to reward, where the uncharted territories of thought are traversed with both bravery and discipline. It is a narrative in which leadership, when coupled with an unwavering commitment to challenging the status quo, can propel entire nations and industries towards new horizons.

And so, as we stand on the precipice of future challenges and opportunities, it is incumbent upon us to internalise the lessons of history. The narrative of innovation, from the somber reflections of the Commonitorium to the relentless defiance of Galileo, from Machiavelli's complex blueprint of power to Schumpeter's dynamic reinterpretation of economic progress, reminds us of one immutable truth: that to lead is to innovate. In leadership, as in all things, there is an inherent tension between the desire to maintain the comfort of the known and the need to reach out into the vast expanse of the unknown. Yet it is precisely this tension that fuels progress, that drives the quest for solutions that can redefine our world.

Inclusive of every whispered warning against unbridled novelty and every bold stroke of genius that defied convention, the arc of human progress is one of perpetual transformation. The meditations of early Christian monks, with their calls to cherish antiquity, find their echo in the modern insistence that together we must steward our knowledge and skills across domains, partners, and generations. These same voices reverberate in the corridors of power at DARPA and in the boardrooms of companies striving to remain competitive in an ever-evolving marketplace. In every instance, the challenge has been the same: to harness innovation as the engine of progress and to lead with vision and determination into new realms of possibility.

As we look to the future, the lessons of this long and storied journey continue to hold immense relevance. The world is once again at a crossroads where the interplay between tradition and innovation will determine the paths we follow. Leadership, in its truest form, is about recognising when to preserve the wisdom of the past and when to break free from its confines to embrace novel ideas that promise a brighter future. Leaders today must, therefore, become not only custodians of established knowledge but also bold pioneers who are unafraid to question and redefine it. They must cultivate environments where risk is managed intelligently, and where breakthrough innovations are pursued with the clarity and purpose that such moments demand.

In the final analysis, the story of innovation is as much a story of leadership as it is of discovery. Whether it is in the measured counsel of ancient doctrine, the revolutionary insights of early modern scientists, the calculated risks of Renaissance political thought, or the high-stakes gambles made in modern innovation hubs, the message remains unaltered: the fortunes of societies are shaped by those who dare to lead by challenging the status quo. It is through such leadership that innovation can thrive, unencumbered by the inertia of outdated conventions, imbued with the audacity to reimagine the possible.

Thus, as we stand here today on the threshold of new challenges – facing issues ranging from environmental uncertainty to the demands of global connectivity and national security – the call to innovate is as urgent as ever. In the culmination of this long journey, from the reflective halls of early Christian thought to the dynamic frontiers of DARPA's research, we are reminded that every great leap forward starts with a spark of insight, a willingness to defy convention, and a leadership that dares to steer the course of history. Let us then honour the legacy of those who came before and embrace the mantle of leadership in our own time, forging ahead with a spirit of creative defiance, guided by the wisdom of the ages and the promise of a better tomorrow.

In this spirit of bold leadership, we come to understand that innovation is not merely a means to an end but rather the very essence of progress and growth. It is the lifeblood that drives our ability to overcome obstacles, reimagine our realities, and build systems that empower us to navigate the complexities of a globalised, interconnected future. As we embark on new projects, taking lessons from DARPA's extraordinary journey, we grasp that leadership is about bringing together diverse talents, harnessing the power of collaborative efforts, and setting the pace for industries and societies alike.

Looking back over centuries of human endeavour, from the contemplative caution of the early Commonitorium to the revolutionary challenges posed by dynamic modern science, we see that each era has been defined by its leaders. Leaders who, in defying established norms and reinterpreting the value of tradition, have paved the way for new ideas to flourish. They are the architects of change, the torchbearers who light the way in dark times and inspire future generations to reach ever higher. Today, as we face our own unique set of challenges, the responsibility of leadership calls upon us to embrace this legacy with both humility and ambition.

In the final reckoning, our journey through the ages reaffirms that innovation and leadership are inextricably linked. The most celebrated innovations are those that have been propelled by leaders who were unafraid to take risks, who understood that progress rarely comes without disruption, and who recognised that the future is built not on the linear continuity of the past but on the creative synthesis of diverse insights and experiences. It is this intertwining of innovation with thoughtful, visionary leadership that continues to define the highest achievements of human endeavours.

And so, as we step forward into an uncertain yet profoundly promising future, we carry with us the lessons of the ages. We honour the measured wisdom of early tradition, the daring experiments of scientific trailblazers, and the relentless drive of modern institutions that refuse to be confined by conventional limits. In doing so, we not only ensure that innovation remains the heartbeat of progress but also that leadership - dynamic, courageous, and deeply responsive to the needs of an ever-changing world - guides us into new realms of possibility.

In the grand narrative of human development, innovation has served as the beacon that illuminates the path forward, even when that path winds through the dark and tumultuous corridors of history. From the ancient days of seeking divine guidance to the modern quest for scientific breakthroughs, innovation has always carried within it the seeds of transformation and renewal. It is a legacy of endless curiosity, unwavering determination, and a keen awareness that every challenge presents an opportunity for reinvention. At its highest, innovation is achieved when it is infused with leadership that not only envisions a better future but also galvanises others to strive toward that vision.

This is the timeless story of human aspiration: a story of individuals and institutions that, when faced with the unknown, have dared to chart a course through the turbulent seas of change; a story where tradition meets transformation, and the ancient wisdom of the past is woven seamlessly into the innovative fabric of the future. And as the torchbearers of this enduring quest, we must ever be mindful of the profound truth that leadership, in its most enlightened form, is the art of marrying preservation with progress, of honouring what has been and shaping what will be.

Thus, as we look forward into the next chapters of our collective journey, we need to commit to leading with both courage and compassion. We need to harness the power of innovation to solve the complex problems of our time, build bridges between disparate ideas, and create a future that is as inclusive as it is advanced. For in the end, it is the union of visionary leadership and relentless innovation that holds the promise not only of a transformed society but of a world where every new idea, every daring experiment, and every meticulous plan contributes to the ever-evolving tapestry of human achievement.

In this grand endeavour, each of us is called to be both an innovator and a leader - a steward of the past and an architect of the future. From the hallowed wisdom of early doctrinal reflections to the explosive breakthroughs heralded by DARPA, our shared history is a reminder that the march of progress is ceaseless, driven by those who dare to imagine, to challenge, and to lead. And it is in this spirit, drawing strength from centuries of hard-won insight and the tireless energy of forward-looking pioneers, that we step boldly into tomorrow, ready to forge new paths, empower diverse voices, and shape a destiny defined by the continuous interplay of tradition and innovation.

In truth, the story of human advancement is not merely a chronicle of isolated events or singular achievements. It is the grand, unending saga of leaders and innovators - of visionary thinkers who, with unwavering resolve, dared to dream of a better world and then set about making that dream real. And as we embrace our role in this unfolding narrative, we must remember that the same principles that guided Galileo and the Médici, that animated Machiavelli's revolutionary insights, that inspired Schumpeter's dynamic theories, continue to light the way for us today. It is this enduring commitment to transcendence - this belief that no challenge is insurmountable and no problem too complex - that remains the true hallmark of leadership and innovation alike.

May we, then, continue in this tradition, nurturing a culture where every challenge is met with insightful creativity and every opportunity for progress is seized with unyielding determination. For it is only through such leadership, intertwined with the spirit of innovation, that we will continue to transform our world, creating legacies that will shine brightly for generations to come.

II

Energy - Navigating Disruption

4
A Short History of Energy Transitions

Long before the advent of steam engines, electricity and the sophisticated energy systems we depend on today, there was an epoch when the entire spectrum of energy required for life's pursuits could be harnessed solely through the sheer physical strength of human or animal muscle. In those early, halcyon days, every stride taken, every burden borne, and every task accomplished was powered directly by the living force within flesh and blood. Imagine for a moment a world where progress was measured in the beating of hearts and the steady rhythm of footsteps, not in the engineered wonders of later centuries. The energy provided by these organic powerhouses was not the refined, mechanised force of technology; rather, it was primal, raw, and intimately interwoven with the rhythms of nature itself.

The discovery of fire, however, marked humanity's first grand conquest of energy beyond the physical might of muscles. Fire, with its dancing flames and unpredictable temperament, could be both a nurturing friend and a daunting adversary. The earliest members of our species who learned how to coax nature's wildest element into submission must have felt an almost divine empowerment. Picture a primitive hearth on a chilly night, the fire crackling and roaring, its warmth banishing the bitter cold and its glow transforming the darkness into a canvas of comforting light. This elemental force, though capricious, allowed early humans to cook their food – a process that not only delightfully transformed raw sustenance into nourishing meals but also served as a vital shield against diseases that might have otherwise ravaged unheated, raw diets. In this sense, fire was not a mere luxury but a necessity; it was energy in its most essential form, one that directly sustained life and ensured survival against the backdrop of a hostile natural world.

Yet, as history often reminds us, progress is an ever-restless force. The reliability of muscle and fire, though invaluable, quickly proved insufficient to meet the burgeoning needs of human societies. With the swift march of time came the realisation that while fire was a masterful ally in the early days of civilisation, its fickle nature meant that it could not solely be depended upon for the grand scale endeavours necessary for the growth of complex societies. The inherent limitations of these early energy sources set the stage for transformative shifts, sparks that would eventually ignite revolutions across history.

The profound transformation began with the advent of agriculture – a transition that reshaped not only energy systems but also the very fabric of society. Although today it might be hard to appreciate just how revolutionary this step was, the decision to employ the strength of animal labour in tandem with human effort was nothing short of a historical inflection point. Imagine a time when communities were nomadic, perpetually on the move and engaged in the ceaseless chase for sustenance that lay scattered across vast, untamed landscapes. Then came the innovative notion of domesticating and harnessing large beasts, such as oxen, to pull ploughs through soil; a decision that, while seemingly modest, heralded an explosion in productivity and stability. This was the era when the subtle interplay of human ingenuity and animal power sowed the seeds of civilisation, liberating countless hands from the immediate rigours of subsistence and allowing them to engage in creative and specialised endeavours.

Communities, now able to settle in one location, began the slow but steady process of cultural, social, and economic evolution. Villages blossomed into thriving settlements, each one brimming with a newfound purpose as people discovered that the harnessing of energy could do much more than simply sustain life – it could launch it into a realm of boundless possibility. Agriculture, bolstered by animal power, was not just a means of survival but also a conduit for innovation. Fields cultivated by ploughs drawn by steadfast oxen yielded bountiful harvests that allowed societies to flourish, setting in motion a chain reaction of economic and cultural specialisation that had profound implications for every aspect of life.

However, the enhanced productivity brought on by the agricultural revolution was not without its constraints. As communities grew larger and ambitions expanded, the limits of energy provided by human and animal muscle were soon reached. It was during this period of mounting need that nature herself presented new solutions, in the form of water and wind. Over countless generations, the resourcefulness of the ancients shone through as they sought to harness the ceaseless flow of rivers and the invisible might of the wind.

Their endeavours were both courageous and ingenious, as they devised methods to direct these natural forces for practical purposes such as grinding grain, pumping water, and even propelling early vessels across serene lakes and vast waterways.

The Romans, those illustrious engineers of antiquity, made monumental strides by perfecting water wheels that turned mills with an impressive efficiency previously unimagined. These water-powered mills became the industrial precursors to the mechanised factories of later ages, their rhythmic turning a constant reminder that energy could be tamed from the natural elements. In parallel, in regions where water proved a scarce resource, the Persians and the Chinese experimented with and refined windmills, structures that, though relying on the capricious breezes, provided a vital alternative to the strength of muscle and the unpredictable nature of fire. Yet even as these innovations ushered in exciting new possibilities, they were accompanied by an inherent fragility – a fragility born from nature's indisputable authority over its own realms. Rivers only flowed where the geography allowed, and the winds, though often generous, were as unreliable as they were capricious. Nevertheless, these pioneering adaptations set the groundwork for the eventual emergence of large-scale energy transitions, illustrating that even the mightiest of human endeavours must often bow in reverence to the laws of nature.

For countless centuries thereafter, wood reigned supreme as the primary energy source underpinning civilisation's expansion. Harvested from vast forests and renewable in nature – at least in theory – wood provided the steady fuel that powered everything from the humble hearth to the blazing forge. However, as the reach of burgeoning empires extended across continents, the once limitless bounty of timber began to dwindle. Entire forests were felled to make way for expanding settlements, defensive fortifications, and imperial industries. In this way, wood, while renewable, became a scarce luxury as the relentless march of progress demanded ever more fuel.

A turning point in this long saga of energy evolution occurred in early 16th-century England. In the 1530s, on the very cusp of monumental change, the nation found itself at a critical juncture. King Henry VIII, a monarch whose reign was as influential as it was tumultuous, had already shaken the foundations of both spiritual and temporal authority by defiantly clashing with the Pope. His infamous quest for a divorce from Catherine of Aragon had sent tremors through the corridors of Christendom, altering the balance of power in Europe. Yet, it was not solely his religious defiance that would carve a new path for England's energy future – it was his sharp economic manoeuvres that laid the seeds of an unexpected revolution.

The dissolution of the monasteries, instigated by Henry's fervent desire for wealth and dominion, proved to be a transformative act on multiple levels. Monasteries, those bastions of faith, learning, and tradition, also controlled vast swathes of land rich in natural resources. Their sudden confiscation meant that lands once sacred not only in spiritual terms but also in economic value were now available for secular use. Many of these lands were replete with untapped mineral wealth, most notably coal – a resource that, until then, had been used sporadically and with limited purpose. Coal, stored beneath the earth like a sleeping giant, was about to be awakened and thrust into the fore as a key player in the burgeoning industrial landscape.

Henry VIII was a man of decisive actions and definite ambitions – half-measures were not in his lexicon. Once a devout Catholic who had in his day penned vehement arguments against Martin Luther's reformation, earning for himself the title 'Defender of the Faith', his views would soon pivot to reflect his own self-interest. When Rome refused to grant him an annulment, Henry severed England's ties with the papacy, declaring himself the Supreme Head of the Church of England. This act of spiritual and political defiance was accompanied by judgements that were as severe as they were transformative. The wealthy monasteries of northern England, many of which were nestled above coal-rich seams, were promptly re-assigned to noble families and crown-loyal businessmen. In doing so, a mineral hitherto considered only in meagre domestic contexts began its long ascent into economic prominence.

The decision to repurpose vast tracts of monastery-owned land had far-reaching implications, as it coincided with a period when the traditional energy resource – wood – was rapidly becoming scarce. With the extensive deforestation brought on by centuries of relentless demand, the price of firewood soared, and its availability dwindled. By the time Queen Elizabeth I ascended to the throne in 1558, the urgency for alternative fuels had grown markedly. Elizabeth herself, inheriting a nation deeply fractured by religious strife, economic pressures, and external threats from a resurgent Catholic Europe, was well aware that survival depended on adaptation and pragmatism. Under her shrewd reign, coal swiftly emerged as a commodity of critical importance.

As London expanded – its streets thick with commerce and its population burgeoning – the diminishing forests could no longer adequately meet the city's energy needs. With the steady decline of wood supplies, coal, particularly that sourced from the coalfields of Newcastle, became indispensable. From modest beginnings as a resource for rudimentary domestic heating, coal evolved into the lifeblood of an increasingly industrial society. The skyline of London, once punctuated by the gentle flicker of wood fires and chimney smoke, began to transform markedly as coal steadily took over. The familiar, comforting sight of woodsmoke was gradually replaced by the pervasive, dark plume of coal smoke, which now blanketed the city as an emblem of the new industrial order.

Yet, not every innovation is met with immediate acceptance, and the transition to coal was no exception. As with all significant shifts in long-established norms, there arose a chorus of dissent from traditionalists who clung steadfastly to the old ways. Critics lamented the rise of the so-called 'sea coal' – a term born out of early encounters with imported coal that carried an unpleasant, sulphurous odour. Its smell and perceived impurity spurred a cautious resistance among those who were privy to the halcyon days of timbered warmth. James I, ascending the throne after Elizabeth, was among those who harboured a deep-seated scepticism towards this new fuel. Of Scottish descent and a man of learned pursuits, James was not blinded by pragmatism alone; he also possessed a genuine concern for the well-being of his subjects, particularly in the face of burgeoning urban pollution. In an attempt to mitigate the noxious effects of coal's fumes, he issued a series of proclamations intended to restrict its use. Yet, despite these regal efforts, the inexorable force of economic necessity proved powerful beyond measure.

Indeed, as the cost of timber soared further amid dwindling

supplies and as coal proved to be a vastly more convenient resource, it entrenched its status as England's primary energy source. By the close of the 17th century and well into the dawn of the 18th, the ripple effects of these early decisions were evident throughout British society. Economic landscapes were reshaped, manufacturing processes overhauled, and a new social order began to emerge – one in which energy itself was the great engine of progress.

As Britain moved into the 18th century, the energy revolution gained momentum with unparalleled force. The Industrial Revolution was not a sudden leap but rather a gradual transformation that had been sowing seeds for centuries. Coal, once a resource relegated to limited domestic uses, had by now blossomed into an industrial powerhouse. By 1700, the population of Britain was expanding rapidly, and its industries – increasingly mechanised and urbanised – required vast amounts of energy to sustain their growth. The coal mines, once mere curiosities, had begun to proliferate across the landscape. To support this industrial behemoth, railways – initially primitive and rudimentary – were constructed with the singular purpose of moving coal from deep within the earth to the ever-growing urban centres. By the year 1760, on the threshold of an industrial age defined by steam and machinery, coal was responsible for nearly two-thirds of England's total energy consumption.

The extraordinary transformation that had been set in motion centuries earlier by the economic manoeuvres of Henry VIII was now in full swing. England, a nation once powered by muscle and fire, had transitioned into a society fuelled by the dark, potent energy of coal. This metamorphosis was not merely an economic shift; it was a reordering of society itself.

Factories sprang up, their hulking shapes silhouetted against a smog-filled sky, and coal-fired steam engines became the beating heart of a rapidly industrialising nation. The labour of millions now revolved around these mechanical marvels, and the very meaning of work was redefined. In an age where traditional agrarian roles gave way to the demands of industrial production, people were inexorably drawn into the rhythms of the machine.

Yet no transformation is without its price. The ascent of coal as the primary energy source carried with it a litany of unforeseen consequences. The mines, often dark and treacherous, became sites of great peril; more than a million individuals laboured in these subterranean labyrinths by the late 19th century. The spectre of mining accidents loomed large, and the illness known as black lung – a grim testament to the harsh realities of working in coal dust – cast a long shadow over those who dared enter the depths. Furthermore, as entire cities mushroomed with the newfound promise of industrial prosperity, the relentless march of urbanisation gave rise to unprecedented levels of pollution. Buildings, once adorned with clean facades, were now festooned with soot and grime – stark symbols of an era where progress was paid for in the tokens of health and environmental degradation.

Nevertheless, even in the face of these dire costs, coal maintained its pre-eminence as the engine of progress for many decades. Its reign, however, was not destined to be eternal. The 20th century signalled the rise of new players in the energy game, as oil and gas began to emerge on the world stage. These new fuels, with their own distinct advantages and challenges, slowly started to usurp the role that coal had long enjoyed. The global energy landscape, once dominated by the dark power of coal, was beginning to show signs of transformation. And yet, this was not a swift or smooth passage; rather, it was a gradual, almost imperceptible shift, much like the slow-burning coal revolution that had dramatically altered England's fate in the 16th century.

As the decades passed and technology advanced, evidence of change manifested in incremental yet pivotal innovations. In 1927, even as coal's influence on global energy remained dominant, the first commercial wind turbine was introduced – a faint hint of the storms of change gathering strength on the horizon. The humble wind turbine, capturing the airy whispers of the breeze and converting them into usable power, foreshadowed a future where renewable energy might once again challenge the might of fossil fuels. This was followed in 1935 by a marvel of engineering and ambition: the Hoover Dam. Standing as a monumental testament to the potential of hydropower, the dam harnessed the immense force of water, redistributing energy in a manner that had rarely been conceived before. And just a few decades later, in 1958, another watershed moment arrived when the first solar-powered satellite was launched into space – an event that echoed with the startling audacity of Henry VIII's earlier defiance of ecclesiastical authority.

Each of these milestones, achieved with the goose-step of progress and the cumulative ingenuity of generations, contributed incrementally to a burgeoning momentum. Decade after decade, the world witnessed the slow but inexorable build-up of a shift toward alternative energy sources. Fast forward to the 21st century, and we find ourselves once again standing at the precipice of a monumental transformation. Renewables

– energy sources such as wind, solar, and hydropower that had once been dismissed as impractical – have steadily evolved into viable, competitive alternatives to the fossil fuels that have underpinned century-long industrial progress. In 2021 alone, global investments in energy transition technologies reached a staggering US$755 billion, a number that speaks volumes about the urgent recognition of an existential imperative.

However, this new transition is unlike the gradual shift from wood to coal that unfurled over centuries. Today's move from fossil fuels to renewable energy is imbued with urgency and existential necessity. The United Nations has warned that to achieve net zero emissions, the world must mobilise an astronomical US$125 trillion by 2050. Such figures dwarf even the most extravagant ambitions of historical monarchs or industrial titans. Yet, as history has repeatedly shown, energy transitions rarely follow a linear trajectory. The seizure of monastic lands by Henry VIII was never conceived as an environmental strategy, nor did James I's scepticism about coal's utility manage to halt its inevitable rise. Rather, societies have a way of adapting when necessity dictates, regardless of how hesitant established institutions may be to embrace change.

In pondering the path ahead, one is drawn to reflect upon the perspective of the past – of those who wielded the rudimentary forces of fire and muscle, of the ingenious farmers who harnessed the ox to plough the fields, and of the visionary engineers who tamed the chaotic gales of water and wind. Each of these pioneers was presented with a choice: to clamor for the familiarity of the old ways or to embrace an uncertain, yet promising, new paradigm. Their decisions, taken in the crucible of necessity and ambition, collectively shaped the course of human civilisation. Today, as we face an energy transition that must not unfold over centuries but within a few decisive decades, the echoes of their choices are felt more strongly than ever.

The challenges that lie ahead are monumental. Unlike previous eras where the consequences of energy transitions could be borne by societies evolving at a more measured pace, modern civilisation is confronted with a crisis that is both global and urgent. Climate change, environmental degradation, and unsustainable consumption have brought us to a crossroads where the luxury of gradual progress is no longer an option. The lessons of history are clear: energy transitions are complex, multifaceted endeavours that ripple outwards, affecting every facet of economic, social, and political life. Yet, like the innovations of the past, they also carry the promise of renewal and rebirth. As new technologies emerge and old habits are challenged, there is hope that a new, sustainable energy future can take shape – one that honours the legacy of progress while forging a path towards conservation and resilience.

The trajectory of the energy revolution is a saga of human ingenuity intertwined with the inexorable laws of nature. In each pivotal moment – from that ancient love affair with fire to the grand exploitation of coal reserves – humankind has both adapted to and shaped the world around it. The dissolution of the monasteries under Henry VIII, an act born of political and economic ambition rather than environmental foresight, inadvertently unlocked the potential for coal to become the driving force of industrialisation. In doing so, it set in motion a chain reaction that would ultimately elevate Britain from a land of wandering tribes and agrarian communities to a nation at the forefront of industrial might. Yet, every new dawn in energy history is invariably accompanied by challenges and sacrifices.

The rapid ascent of coal propelled the very concept of labour into a new era. As factories rose, powered by the relentless churn of coal-fired steam engines, traditional patterns of work were upended. The pastoral idyll of agrarian communities gave way to the relentless pace of urban industry, where labourers worked long hours under harsh and often perilous conditions. The prosperity that accompanied this industrial boom was shadowed by the human cost extracted from the depths of treacherous mines and the polluted urban landscapes that emerged as a bitter by-product of progress. Societies were transformed, not merely by the technologies they embraced, but by the social and moral dilemmas that ensued.

In considering the broader historical arc, it becomes evident that energy transitions do more than simply change the means of production; they reshape the very character of society. The evolution from wood to coal, and from coal to oil and gas, was not a linear series of technological upgrades. Each shift was accompanied by profound changes in economic structures, social hierarchies, and even cultural identities. The very essence of work, leisure, and community was redefined by the forces that powered these transitions. Factories not only reconfigured the physical landscape but also heralded a new social order – one where urbanisation, industrialisation, and modern economic theory converged to create both unprecedented prosperity and profound new challenges.

Yet, despite the formidable setbacks and the widespread apprehension that accompanied each new technological era, progress persisted. With each new energy source harnessed, the ingenuity of humankind shone through like a beacon, illuminating the pathways to adaptation and reinvention. The coal era, for instance, though fraught with pollution and public health challenges, laid the groundwork for the modern industrial society. It propelled economic growth at a rate previously unimagined, catapulting Britain to the forefront of global commerce and setting the stage for technological innovations that continue to shape our world today.

Now, as we stand at the threshold of yet another transformative period powered by renewable energy, the lessons of the past resonate with haunting clarity. Our modern civilisation is challenged by a crisis that, while different in its technological underpinnings, shares much in common with the struggles of earlier epochs. Just as the early hunter mastered fire, and the agrarian society embraced the caldron of agriculture, so too must we now muster the collective will and ingenuity required to transition from fossil fuels to sustainable, renewable energy sources. The stakes are higher than ever – not merely a question of economic convenience, but one of survival for our planet and future generations.

Already, the runway towards change is visibly unfolding. The global economy is beginning to pivot away from its entrenched dependence on fossil fuels, driven by both technological breakthroughs and an urgent environmental imperative. Every new wind turbine that rises against the horizon, every solar array glinting under the sun, and every hydroelectric dam harnessing the kinetic energy of water is a symbol of the forward march of progress. Investments in renewable technology are soaring. Governments across the globe, in tandem with the private sector, are charting ambitious paths to reduce carbon footprints and embrace cleaner, more sustainable forms of energy. Yet, this transition is not without its challenges. The infrastructure overhaul required to supplant centuries-old systems is immense, and the need for rapid adaptation – economically, socially, and politically – is undeniable.

History teaches us that such transformations happen not in fits and starts, but in steady, determined steps. Over the centuries, the energy transitions that have defined our progress were not sudden epiphanies; they were the cumulative result of incremental innovations, political decisions, and collective will. The momentous shift towards renewable energy may indeed be precipitated by urgency, but it is also the inevitable consequence of human resilience and the relentless pursuit of a better future. Consequently, as we look to the challenges ahead, it is vital to draw inspiration from the countless generations who have navigated similar cross-roads in times past.

The tale of energy evolution is one of audacious vision, relentless endeavour, and the resilience of the human spirit. Whether it was the primitive control of fire that afforded early humans a shield against nature's brutal chill or the decisive, if unexpected, land seizures of Henry VIII that set the stage for England's industrial might, each chapter in this ongoing saga is interwoven with stories of adaptation and survival. Today, the energy transition unfolding before us is not merely a shift in our methods of powering our lives – it is a profound transformation that will shape every facet of our socio-economic and environmental existence.

Consider the early agriculturists, who, upon realising the benefits of harnessing animal strength, shifted their lifestyles from nomadic existence to settled civilisation. Their decision, simple yet transformative, unlocked unprecedented levels of efficiency and stability. It allowed for the accumulation of surplus, the development of specialised trades, and arguably, the very birth of civilisation as we know it. In these past decisions lie invaluable lessons for our time – lessons about the importance of adaptation, the need to balance tradition with innovation, and the perennial truth that progress, however disruptive, paves the way for future prosperity.

As we stand on the brink of a revolutionary moment in energy history – the moment when renewables may finally supplant fossil fuels – we are reminded that our forebears faced similar crossroads. The choices made by that early farmer, the determined engineer, and even the embattled monarch were not driven solely by a desire for comfort or luxury. They were, as much as our own decisions must be today, driven by necessity – the unyielding imperative to adapt or perish. In an age where the consequences of inaction could be catastrophic, the pathway forward must be one of decisive, collective commitment to sustainable change.

Looking ahead, the transformation from an energy landscape dominated by coal, oil, and gas to one powered by renewable sources is not just an environmental imperative; it is also a matter of economic renaissance and social justice. The same inexorable forces that once propelled the Industrial Revolution – innovation, investment, and the drive for progress – are now being harnessed to forge a cleaner, more sustainable future. Governments, communities, and industries must, with the urgency bred by our current challenges, collaborate to ensure that this transition is both swift and inclusive, preventing the hard choices that past generations had to make while shouldering the burdens of pollution, inequality, and environmental degradation.

In this new era, technological advancement is already reconfiguring the energy landscape. The rapid integration of digital technologies, improved energy storage solutions, and groundbreaking innovations in solar, wind, and hydropower are coalescing to form the backbone of a modern energy system that is both resilient and adaptive. With every new installation of a solar panel or wind turbine, humanity asserts its capacity to redefine the boundaries of what is possible. The commitment is not merely to replace old fuels with new; it is to fundamentally rethink our relationship with energy, ensuring that in doing so we cultivate a sustainable future for all.

Yet, challenges persist. Transitioning an entire economy from fossil fuels to renewables is a task of unprecedented scale – one that requires international co-operation, extensive planning, and immense investment. The numbers are staggering, with global estimates suggesting that trillions of dollars will be needed to create the infrastructure required for a sustainable energy future. But, if history has taught us anything, it is that even the most formidable obstacles can be overcome when necessity becomes the mother of invention. As was the case in every previous energy transition, once the commitment is made and the collective will is mobilised, innovation follows, and society adapts.

In reflecting upon this narrative of energy evolution – from the early defiance of nature's elements to the world-altering consequences of monarchial decrees – one sees clearly that each era of change was propelled not by isolated decisions but by the cumulative weight of necessity, vision, and collective endeavour. Just as the oxen that toiled in the fields once heralded the transformation of society, so too must our modern commitment to renewable energy serve as a testament to our capacity for change. The journey from relying on muscle and fire to harnessing the power of coal, and then to embracing the clean promise of renewables, is an odyssey that underscores both the fragility and the resilience of human civilisation.

As we face the challenges of the 21st century, it becomes increasingly apparent that the lessons of the past hold the keys to our future. The energy transitions of yore, marked by both triumph and tribulation, provide a roadmap for navigating the complexities and uncertainties of our own time. While the technological landscape has evolved dramatically, the fundamental principles remain unchanged: adaptation is essential, innovation is inevitable, and the demands of survival will always drive us to reimagine the way we harness the forces of nature.

Today, as political leaders, industrialists, and citizens come together to confront the profound issues of climate change and environmental degradation, we must ask ourselves: how quickly can we embrace this new energy reality? The pace of change in previous eras may have been measured over centuries, but the current challenges demand a transformation that takes place within a few decades. The fate of our planet – its climate, its ecosystems, and the well-being of its inhabitants – hinges upon the decisions we make now. In this light, the history of energy transitions becomes not just a chronicle of human ingenuity, but a clarion call to action for our time.

In conclusion, the saga of energy from the raw, untamed power of muscle and fire to the commanding dominance of coal – and now, to the hopeful promise of renewables – is a testament to the ceaseless ingenuity of human civilisation. It is a reminder that every pivotal moment in our past was driven by the uncompromising need to adapt and flourish, regardless of the challenges posed by the forces of nature or the inertia of tradition. As we forge ahead into an uncertain future, let us draw inspiration from the early pioneers of our civilisation, those brave souls who, in the face of overwhelming odds, dared to dream and, in doing so, laid the foundations of a modern world.

The energy transition we face today, much like those that preceded it, is a journey of transformation, innovation, and survival. It calls upon us to harness our collective will and to invest in a future where progress is measured not simply by economic growth, but by the harmony between humanity and the natural world. Let the story of past transitions – from the flicker of fire that once lit the corridors of prehistoric caves to the mighty coal-powered engines that ignited the Industrial Revolution – serve as a beacon of hope and a pragmatic guide. For in every epoch, when faced with the imperatives of necessity, humanity has risen to the challenge, reimagining its destiny with courage, ingenuity, and an unwavering resolve.

As we embark on this new chapter of energy evolution, let the memory of early human endeavours inspire us to embrace a future powered by renewable energy – one that promises not only to safeguard our environment but also to ensure a legacy of innovation and sustainability for generations yet unborn. The journey ahead is fraught with challenges as daunting as those faced by our ancestors, but it is also filled with opportunities to redefine what is possible. The choices we make in the coming decades will shape the destiny of our planet in ways that echo far beyond the boundaries of time, forging a legacy that future historians will one day recount as another magnificent chapter in the unyielding saga of human progress.

Thus, as we stand amidst the flickering shadows of coal-fired memories and gaze upon the bright promise of renewable energy, we must ask ourselves: how swiftly will we act, and how deeply will we commit? The historical fabric of our civilisation, woven with the threads of countless energy transitions, compels us to answer this question not with hesitation, but with resolve. For the survival of our planet, and indeed our very way of life, depends on our collective ability to harness the infinite potential of nature in a manner that is both sustainable and just.

In drawing these threads together, let it be remembered that the grand narrative of energy is not solely a chronicle of technological marvels; it is also a story of human resilience, adaptation, and hope. Just as the steady beat of the ox and the crackle of the primitive flame once paved the way for civilisation's rise, so too will the clean, steady hum of renewable energy herald a new era of prosperity and environmental stewardship. The road ahead is long and challenging, demanding of us the same spirit of bold innovation that has characterised every chapter of our past. And as we write this new chapter, the lessons of history alongside the promise of tomorrow will forever light our path.

In the final analysis, whether it is the splintered remnants of ancient fires, the enduring legacies of coal and steam, or the gleaming future of wind, solar, and water power, the journey of energy is a testament to the indomitable spirit of humankind. It is a narrative of perpetual evolution, a dynamic interplay between human ingenuity and the vast, unyielding forces of nature. As we stand on the brink of a future that demands not merely adaptation but transformation within mere decades, we are reminded that the stars of progress are ignited by the resolve to act and the commitment to a sustainable future. The lessons of the past are clear: history is made by those who dare to change, and the energy transitions of our time will be defined not merely by technological breakthroughs but by the collective will to safeguard our home, our Earth.

And so, as we peek into the uncertain yet promising horizon, let us remember that each revolution in energy has been more than a mere shift in resources – it has been a profound transformation that redefined society, rebuilt economies, and renewed the human spirit. The time to act is now, for the energy transition awaiting us is not just a continuation of history but a bold leap towards a future where human progress and environmental viability walk hand in hand. In embracing this challenge, we honour the legacy of our forebears and embrace the possibility of a brighter, cleaner world for all.

5

Energy Transitions – A Story of Leadership and Betrayal

On a cool autumn evening many years ago, beneath a sky dusted with countless stars, an old storyteller named Edmund gathered a small group of curious listeners around a crackling bonfire. In the flickering light of those humble flames, he began to tell a tale that spanned millennia - a narrative in which energy was not merely a physical force but the lifeblood of human progress, a silent partner in the quest for civilisation and enlightenment. Edmund's voice, steady and measured, carried the listeners back to the first moments when our ancestors discovered the magic of fire. They remembered how, in a time when the world was painted in shades of darkness and mystery, a lone flicker of flame sparked a revolution. That small blaze, rather than being seen as a simple source of warmth or a means to roast the evening's meal, symbolised hope itself - signalling that humankind might indeed harness the raw forces of nature to defy its own inherent limitations.

In this early epoch, when muddy tracks were the only roads and every night was fraught with boundless uncertainties, individuals gathered around the flame and suddenly assumed roles far greater than mere survival. Leaders emerged among these early communities - guardians of the kindling that lit the night, custodians of a fragile future. These were not tyrants bent on hoarding power or wealth; their leadership was soft, shaped by mutual care and collective determination to see each member of the group flourish. Each night, as the fire cast long shadows and wove tales of ancestors past and hopes for tomorrow, those gathered learned that leadership, intertwined with energy, was about more than survival - it was the very foundation upon which progress was built.

Centuries passed, and Edmund's story carried the listeners forward through time. The simple, comforting glow of fire was gradually replaced by new, more potent forms of energy. His narrative meandered through the ancient transformation of wood into charcoal, then led to the revelation that coal, hidden in the deep embrace of the earth, could be extracted and harnessed to warm entire communities. In eighteenth-century England, where vast, emerald forests once sprawled across the land were now dwindling and firewood had become a precious resource, coal emerged as a boon. It offered an abundant alternative, lighting up grim factories and powering the engines that would reshape the landscape of society. The transformation sparked by coal was nothing short of revolutionary. Steam engines roared to life, smokestacks punctuated the horizon, and cities, like burgeoning behemoths, expanded at an unprecedented pace. Yet, as the listeners learned in Edmund's tale, every moment of transformational progress carried with it a cascade of challenges and questions about who would lead society into this brave new realm.

It was not merely the invention of new machines or the discovery of resource-rich seams in the earth that pressed thinkers to reconsider their understanding of leadership. With every emerging form of energy came the haunting questions: Who would steer society through such radical metamorphosis? How could these raw, untamed powers be guided to serve the common good rather than to enrich a privileged few? Edmund recalled the story of William Stanley Jevons, a keen economist of the 19th century, who uncovered a paradox that echoed through the ages. As coal-powered steam engines improved in efficiency, it was expected that reduced consumption would follow, sparing precious resources. Yet, contrary to such hopes, a surge in overall usage was observed - a phenomenon that would later be known as the Jevons Paradox. The very efficiencies brought by the innovations in steam technology had a perverse effect, encouraging an ever greater demand for coal as industry and commerce boomed. As the narrative unfolded, Edmund stressed that this paradox was not simply a matter of economics; it was a lesson in humility for human inventiveness, a reminder that progress often comes with unforeseen costs. Innovation could indeed lead to enhancements, yet it might also spur greater appetites, a pattern that would repeat itself in every age.

As his listeners sat enraptured around the bonfire, the narrative took a leap into the modern day - a time when the world teetered on the brink of another transformative energy transition. This transition, unlike those of the past that were confined to shifting sources of power, represented a profound rethinking of not only how energy was produced but also how it was distributed and consumed. The modern landscape was one of incredible promise, riddled with challenges unlike any before. The dual threats of climate change and resource depletion loomed large over every political debate and economic plan. Edmund's eyes glistened as he described this era as one that demanded not just technical ingenuity, but also visionary leadership. Leaders of this modern age were called upon to balance immediate economic demands with the long-term imperative of sustainability. It was a time when the ancient wisdom of philosophers such as Aristotle found new resonance. Aristotle had long maintained that the highest aspiration of human life was not survival alone but the achievement of eudaimonia - a state of flourishing marked by virtue, wisdom, and purpose. In the context of the modern energy revolution, this wisdom suggested that the ultimate goal in policy and practice should be to create an environment where people and the planet could truly flourish, rather than merely pursuing economic metrics.

The narrative then shifted to a striking example of modern moral leadership - the ambitious strides taken by the European Union in its Green Deal. Edmund painted a picture of a union of nations united by a common purpose: to steer their economic and environmental policies towards a sustainable, hopeful future. With its lofty target of carbon neutrality by 2050, the Green Deal was not just a policy plan; it was a philosophical commitment, a pledge that sought to entwine the well-being of citizens and the environment in a harmonious relationship. Yet, Edmund's thoughtful tone did not obscure the formidable difficulties that lay ahead. He recalled that increased efficiency in renewable technologies, while inherently promising, could still lead to greater consumption unless met with rigorous, responsible management. This challenge underlined a timeless truth: that leadership in energy transitions required more than setting ambitious numerical targets – it demand a deep commitment to moral responsibility and ethical frameworks.

Amidst these global endeavours, Edmund's narrative took an unexpected turn, addressing a recent and controversial chapter in the modern energy saga. He spoke passionately of a moment when a powerful nation, long a key player on the international stage, had chosen a path that many saw as a betrayal of global unity. The United States, having once been a beacon of moral leadership in energy policy, had made the singular decision to withdraw from the Paris Accord. In Edmund's tale, this act was far more than a mere shift in political posture – it was a grave misstep, one that cast a long shadow over the collective progress of nations. The Paris Accord had symbolised an extraordinary commitment to curbing climate change and investing in a future where renewables reigned supreme. It was an embodiment of a promise to the next generation, a pledge to take responsibility for the planet's fragile state. To walk away from that responsibility, Edmund argued, was to forsake the very principles of ethical stewardship that humanity had been striving to cultivate across the ages.

In his rich narrative, Edmund described how the withdrawal from the Paris Accord by the United States could be seen as an abandonment of the kind of moral leadership that was vital during energy transitions. He depicted a fictional yet representative scene in which an assembly of global leaders convened in a grand hall, a modern echo of ancient councils gathered by firelight. In that assembly, representatives from every corner of the world spoke of their hopes and fears, of how their societies were being remoulded by new energy paradigms. The European delegates, bolstered by their Green

Deal ambitions, emphasised the need for a united and ethical global approach. Meanwhile, representatives from China, with their long-honoured strategic consistency of energy planning - stretching not over fleeting election cycles but over visionary generations - recounted stories of dramatic progress in renewable capacities. Leaders from local communities, driven by the resurgence of decentralised energy projects, reminded all that the future of energy was not only a matter of technology but one of communal responsibility. Amid these voices of unity, however, the absence of the American delegate was felt as a cold void - a reminder of how a single nation's departure from the Paris collective had undermined the spirit of cooperation and mutual moral accountability. Edmund wove this narrative with the care of a poet, lamenting that while technological progress was being made, the failure to uphold shared commitments could erode the very foundations upon which any sustainable future was to be built.

Drawing on historical analogies, Edmund compared the modern misstep to the ancient lessons of leadership around the campfire, where every flicker of flame signalled not absolute power but a mutual commitment to survival. The US decision to pull out of the Paris Accord was cast as a betrayal of that timeless pact - a refusal to share in the ancient and enduring ideals of stewardship, care, and communal progress. He reminded his listeners that, throughout history, every energy transition had been catalysed by leaders who embraced ethical responsibility. Just as the early guardians protected the flame, so too must modern leaders nurture a legacy that transcends narrow national interests. The abandonment of the Paris Accord, Edmund asserted, had not only jeopardised the collective fight against climate change but had also signalled a retreat from the idea that true leadership was measured by the ability to think beyond immediate gains and to invest in the long-term flourishing of all nations.

Yet the tale was far from dismal; it was interwoven with episodes of hope and promise. Edmund's narrative turned to the inspiring example of China, which had long embraced a long-term strategy in its pursuit of energy leadership. In this part of the story, he recounted how, with unwavering determination, China had transformed itself into a global powerhouse in renewable energy. Over the past few decades, through state-of-the-art investments in solar panels, wind turbines, and battery storage, the nation had reduced its reliance on fossil fuels and emerged as a pioneer of green technology. This consistent, decades-long planning was starkly contrasted with the reactive approaches seen in some Western democracies. Whereas short-term electoral cycles often forced governments to focus on immediate concerns, China's unbroken commitment to forward-thinking energy policies showcased the virtues of long-term planning and moral consistency. Still, even in China's journey, the ever-present paradox of efficiency persisted. The more capable its technological systems became, the more energy was consumed - as if every victory in harnessing nature's power nudged human ambition a step further without sufficient restraint. It was in these moments that Edmund stressed, like in every era, the need for leaders who could balance innovation with conservation, who could ensure that progress never turned into a reckless chase.

While nations and governments played critical roles, Edmund was quick to remind his audience that corporate leaders had an equally weighty responsibility in this sprawling narrative of energy transitions. He recounted the dramatic transformation witnessed in some of the world's largest oil companies. Once titans of fossil fuel dependency, they had begun to pivot towards investments in renewable energy. One such company, known throughout the world by its initials, BP, had rebranded itself as "Beyond Petroleum," signalling an ambitious, if somewhat tentative, foray into cleaner, greener technologies. This transformation was not, however, achieved without internal conflict. Corporate boardrooms, once dominated by the relentless pursuit of immediate profit, were now battlegrounds where visions of short-term financial returns clashed with calls for long-term environmental stewardship. In these high-stakes arenas, the teachings of Aristotle resurfaced as a beacon of hope. True leadership, according to the ancient Greek thinker, was not about accumulating wealth or maximising efficiency; it was about creating conditions that allowed for the flourishing of the human spirit - both within corporations and in the communities that depended on them.

Edmund's narrative found a poignant echo in the story of a small, oil-rich nation that had turned its fortunes towards a sustainable future. He told the tale of Norway, whose people had long prospered on the world stage as major exporters of oil. Rather than allowing this wealth to sow seeds of complacency, Norway had taken a bold, visionary step: it had channelled its oil revenues into establishing a sovereign wealth fund. This fund, in turn, enabled Norway to make significant investments in renewable energy and social welfare programmes, thus forging a path that reconciled economic success with long-term sustainability. Norway's decision was not merely a pragmatic economic strategy; it was a testament to the power of ethical leadership. It was a demonstration that resources, if managed with wisdom and foresight, could be reinvested in a future where prosperity was measured not solely by national coffers but by the quality of life enjoyed by its citizens. Edmund recalled how, in Norway, a high proportion of new car sales were electric, symbolising a genuine commitment to an environmentally sustainable future – a commitment that few nations in the modern era could yet claim.

Yet, just as nations like Norway and China illuminated the path to a sustainable tomorrow, another layer of the modern struggle was unfolding in communities across the globe. Edmund's voice took on a reflective tone as he recounted how decentralised energy systems began to challenge centuries-old power structures. No longer was energy the exclusive domain of vast, centralised power plants or state-controlled monopolies. Instead, communities now took charge of their own energy destiny. In towns and villages scattered across continents, families and local councils alike invested in solar panels, erected wind turbines on open moorlands, and established microgrids that enabled localised, independent generation and consumption of power. These new, decentralised systems were not without their own challenges, however. Local leaders found themselves grappling with the technical and administrative complexities of integrating an array of disparate energy sources into a coherent, efficient grid. Yet, in doing so, they were not merely managing machines and resources – they were redefining what it meant to lead in a world being reshaped by technological progress.

Amid these sweeping changes, another perennial truth reasserted itself: technological advances, though vital, could not alone secure the future of our energy landscape. Edmund emphasised that the interplay between human behaviour and machine efficiency was an enduring theme in the ongoing saga of progress. Despite remarkable breakthroughs in renewable technology, the same tendency towards increased consumption that once had been heralded by the Jevons Paradox continued to loom large. As efficiency improved, the resulting lower energy costs could easily provoke an inadvertent surge in overall consumption - a trend witnessed in modern digital infrastructure, where advances in computer processors and data centres had led to soaring energy demands. It was a sobering reminder that while technology offered mighty tools for harnessing energy, it also demanded a corresponding evolution in human attitudes and habits. Efficiency, if not tempered by responsible management and cultural shifts towards conservation, could very well become a double-edged sword, undermining the very promise of a sustainable future.

In the halls of modern power, as leaders deliberated on policies and practices, the voice of ancient philosophy still echoed. Edmund recalled the timeless words of Aristotle, whose vision of eudaimonia - that profound state of "flourishing" where virtue, reason, and purpose coalesce - served as an enduring benchmark for human achievement. In the narrative of energy transitions, this Aristotelian ideal took on renewed urgency. The true measure of progress was not simply found in economic statistics or the efficiency of new technologies, but in the extent to which innovations enriched lives, nurtured communities, and safeguarded the environment for future generations. Leaders, whether on the grand stage of international diplomacy or in the quiet enclave of a small village, were thus called upon to transcend the narrow confines of immediate self-interest. They needed to embrace a holistic vision - one where every watt of energy produced, every innovative policy enacted, and every technological breakthrough achieved contributed to a broader tapestry of human well-being.

It was in this interconnected web of technology, policy, and human aspiration that the lesson of the Paris Accord resonated with force. Edmund recounted with no small measure of sorrow and indignation the United States' decision to retreat from that global commitment - the Paris Accord. For many, this move symbolised not only a retreat from the responsibility of mitigating climate change but also a failure to recognise the moral imperatives that should underpin energy transitions. United States, in its self-appointed position as a leader on the world stage, had long been expected to champion the cause of global sustainability. Its withdrawal, therefore, was seen as a dramatic abdication of moral leadership - an act that left a void and cast doubt on the global community's ability to cooperate in addressing an existential threat. In Edmund's story, this abandonment was not isolated; it was woven into the broader tapestry of energy transitions as a cautionary tale of what happens when short-term political expediency overrides the long-term moral imperatives of responsible stewardship.

In a vivid reenactment that seemed to leap from the pages of history into the heart of modernity, Edmund described a heated debate held in a grand conference hall filled with emissaries from across the globe. The room buzzed with urgency and determination as leaders presented their visions for a sustainable future. One voice in the assembly – a seasoned diplomat from a European nation with its Green Deal ambitions – forcefully criticised the decision of the US to leave the Paris Accord. The diplomat argued that this withdrawal was more than just a political manoeuvre; it was a repudiation of the basic principles of ethical leadership, a reluctance to shoulder the collective responsibility that every nation must bear in the face of climate change. The passionate outcry resonated deeply with many present, serving as a poignant reminder of the moral dimensions intrinsic to energy policy. As the debate raged on, the void left by the absence of the American delegate was palpably felt, symbolising the broader gap between short-term national interests and the enduring need for a united, morally guided global strategy.

In the wake of such profound debates, corporate leaders were not immune to the call for ethical responsibility. Edmund's narrative took an inspiring turn as he narrated how businesses, traditionally driven by quarterly profits and shareholder demands, were beginning to recognise the vital importance of sustainable practices. Once, the measure of a company's success was its ability to generate immediate financial returns, but the pressure of climate urgency was compelling even the most profit-centric organisations to rethink their strategies. Case after case emerged of corporations shifting their focus from fossil-fuel dependence to a vision of renewable energy, recognising that long-term prosperity depended on environmental stewardship and social responsibility. These internal transformations, however, were not devoid of tension. Boardroom struggles and debates over project funding vividly illustrated the difficulty of reconciling the imperatives of instant profit with the slower, steadier pace of sustainable innovation. Yet, within this corporate milieu, the ancient wisdom of Aristotle stood as a guiding light - a reminder that true leadership was measured by one's commitment to the greater good, to fostering conditions that allowed both people and nature to thrive.

Edmund then turned his attention back to the global stage,

where nations such as Norway provided shining examples of ethical reinvention. Norway, despite its reputation as one of the world's foremost oil exporters, had embraced a bold and transformative policy. Their sovereign wealth fund, constructed from oil revenues, had been rechanneled into investments that spanned renewable energy projects and social welfare initiatives. This strategic reinvestment was a demonstration of moral leadership in action – a declaration that wealth generated from finite resources could – and should – be harnessed to build a sustainable future. Edmund detailed how, in Norway, electric vehicles had become not an anomaly but a widespread reality, with more than eighty per cent of new car sales being electric. This change, he explained, was not simply a matter of technology or market forces; it was the tangible outcome of a leadership philosophy that placed the collective, long-term interest of society above the temptations of immediate gain.

As the timeless narrative wove through epochs – from the mysticism of ancient bonfires to the modern boardrooms where billions of pounds were at stake – the role of decentralised energy systems emerged as a vital new chapter. Edmund described vibrant communities scattered across the globe, from remote villages to bustling urban centres, where the decentralisation of energy was reshaping society. In these microcosms, local residents took charge of establishing their own sustainable energy networks, installing rooftop solar panels, erecting modest wind turbines on available land, and constructing microgrids that allowed them to generate, store, and use renewable energy in an integrated manner. This grassroots revolution was both liberating and challenging. On the one hand, it returned power – both literally and figuratively

– to the people, breaking the monopolistic control held by centralised institutions. On the other, it required local leaders and communities to master the complexities of integrating dispersed energy sources into a coherent whole, ensuring that efficiency, reliability, and fairness were maintained. In many ways, these decentralised networks echoed the ancient gatherings around the campfire – a sharing of resources and collective responsibility that embodied the best of human cooperation.

Yet even as these decentralised models blossomed, the inherent tension between technological progress and human behaviour remained. Although scientists and engineers made tremendous strides in increasing the efficiency of renewable technologies, the shadow of the efficiency paradox loomed large. With every leap forward in technology, there was the risk that the efficiencies achieved would be offset by ever-increasing demand. It was as if the universe itself was challenging humanity to confront its own insatiable drive for progress – a reminder that innovation without a concomitant shift in mindset might ultimately lead to unintended consequences. Edmund's narrative seemed to caution that while embracing new technologies was essential, it was equally crucial to foster cultural changes that promoted conservation and balanced consumption. The promise of renewable energy would remain unfulfilled unless accompanied by a fundamental transformation in how society valued and conserved its resources.

The old storyteller continued, his voice softening as he invoked the ethical framework of Aristotle – a philosopher whose teachings had traversed the centuries to retain their relevance even in an age of high technology and global connectivity. For

Edmund, Aristotle's notion of eudaimonia was not an abstract, lofty ideal but a practical metric against which the progress of modern society should be measured. True progress, he argued, was not merely the accumulation of wealth or the unbridled expansion of industry; it was the ability of a society to foster conditions in which every individual could flourish. In the context of the modern energy revolution, this meant that all efforts to harness new forms of power - be it solar, wind, or any yet-to-be-invented technology - had to serve the larger purpose of human well-being and environmental sustainability. Leaders, whether operating on government stages, in corporate boardrooms, or at the grassroots level, were required to balance their ambitions for growth with a commitment to ethical responsibility. The moral compass provided by ancient philosophy was, in Edmund's view, more necessary than ever.

At length, as the fire's embers began to cool and the night deepened into quiet reflection, Edmund's narrative reached its climax - a sweeping vision of the future that intertwined technology, policy, and moral leadership into a single, cohesive story. In this vision, the global community stood at a crossroads, faced with decisions that would echo throughout the ages. The energy transition before them was not a mere swap of resources but a profound reorganisation of society and economy - a revolution that demanded new ways of thinking about everything from international diplomacy to everyday choices about energy consumption. It required leaders who could see beyond the immediate horizon to recognise that every technological advance, every policy reform, and every innovation in energy production had a ripple effect on the lives of people around the world.

In the dim light of the cooling fire, Edmund recalled that each energy revolution in history had come with its own triumphs and tragedies. The early days of kindling flames had been filled with hope and small acts of communal leadership; the industrial era had shown both the transformative power of coal and the perils of unchecked consumption; the modern shift towards renewables was blessed with remarkable technological achievements yet haunted by the efficiency paradox and marred by moral lapses such as the retreat from the Paris Accord. It was in this complex interplay of ambition and responsibility, of fleeting victories and enduring challenges, that the true test of leadership was found. The leaders of tomorrow, Edmund stressed, would need to embody a synthesis of the virtues of ancient guardians and the innovations of modern scientists - a blend of ethical fortitude and practical ingenuity that could guide humanity through the turbulence of change.

In one particularly vivid passage of his tale, Edmund described an imaginary future montage in which a new generation of leaders emerged from every corner of the world. These leaders gathered in a modern forum, which reminded him strikingly of those ancient councils assembled around the flickering fire. There, young and old alike debated passionately not only technological solutions but also the moral and ethical underpinnings of every decision. They spoke at length about the importance of fostering a culture that valued sustainability over short-term gain, of building societies where every project was scrutinised not only for its economic returns but for its impact on the environment and on human life. In one memorable exchange, a young leader from a previously impoverished region recounted how, despite limited resources, their community had embraced decentralised renewable energy projects as a means of self-determination. This leader emphasised that technology was only as good as the values that guided its application - values that transcended borders and commercial interests. Such stories of grassroots empowerment stood in stark contrast to the narrative of retreat and isolation symbolised so poignantly by the US decision to withdraw from the Paris Accord. According to Edmund, the refusal to take collective moral responsibility had the potential to fracture the global community at a time when unity was more crucial than ever.

Edmund's voice gathered strength as he recounted how the lessons of history were being internalised by those who took up the mantle of leadership across the globe. In boardrooms, in government offices, and even in humble local meeting halls, the call for responsible stewardship was echoing louder than ever before. Leaders began to understand that every decision regarding energy production, every policy that either promoted or inhibited efficiency and sustainability, was imbued with a deeper ethical charge. It was not enough to chase efficiency and innovation for their own sake; every technological breakthrough had to be harnessed cautiously, with an eye toward the collective well-being of humanity and the preservation of the planet. As the modern world stood on the cusp of further revolutions in energy - transformations that promised both unprecedented opportunities and daunting challenges - the need for a moral and visionary leadership had never been clearer.

The narrative continued, delving into the intricacies of policy and governance, exploring how international forums struggled to find common ground in the face of divergent national interests. In these forums, the legacy of the Paris Accord was invoked repeatedly - as a symbol of hope and as a touchstone of moral responsibility. Yet while many nations clung to this ideal, others, swayed by short-term considerations or nationalist sentiments, were tempted to look in the opposite direction. Leaders in Europe, Asia, Africa, and elsewhere echoed these sentiments, argued that success in the energy revolution would depend more on ethical leadership and long-term commitment than on any single nation's transient policies. The debate over the Paris Accord, Edmund noted, thus became a rallying point - a call for moral introspection that resonated across continents and sectors.

As Edmund's tale drew inexorably towards its close, he left his listeners with a vision - a vision in which the future of energy was not merely a matter of exponents and megawatts, but a testament to humanity's capacity for wisdom, cooperation, and moral renewal. In this envisioned future, every new form of energy was embraced as a step towards a more sustainable way of living; every innovation was temperate with the cautious wisdom of those who had learned from centuries of both triumph and error. Leaders, from the highest echelons of government to the local guardians of decentralised energy, would work together not only to harness nature's power but also to build a world where economic success was inextricably linked to the well-being of every individual and every community. The narrative, rich with lessons from ancient guardians to modern reformers, underscored that the true measure of progress was how well humanity could reconcile technological prowess with a deep, abiding sense of responsibility.

In the gentle quiet that followed the conclusion of the story, the fire's glow served as a humble reminder that something as simple as a flame had once ignited the spark of progress, and with it, the enduring hope that each generation could build upon the foundations laid by those who came before. Edmund's tale, spanning from the rudimentary comforts of flickering fires to the sophisticated dance of renewable technologies and international politics, was a plea - a plea for moral leadership in an age defined by transitions and transformations. His story asked, in no uncertain terms, whether modern leaders could rise above fleeting national interests and partisan squabbles to embrace a higher calling - a calling that put the well-being of humanity and the planet above all else.

Now, as the night deepened and the once-roaring bonfire reduced to glowing embers, the gathered listeners sat in reflective silence. They had been taken on a journey across time and space, witnessing how energy had been the grand enabler of human progress; from primitive fires that lit up nightly gatherings to the complex interplay of modern technology and policy. Yet through every epoch, one lesson had shone clear: that leadership is not merely about harnessing power but about nurturing hope. It is about guiding societies through stormy transitions, about making difficult choices for the greater good - even when the choices are fraught with political controversy and personal sacrifice.

The moral of the story, as Edmund gently concluded, was that a nation's legacy is not defined solely by its technological or economic achievements. Rather, it is measured by its willingness to shoulder responsibility, to learn from the past, and to commit wholeheartedly to a future where every individual has the opportunity to thrive. The United States' retreat from the Paris Accord, he warned, was a stark reminder that even the mightiest of nations could falter if they failed to embrace this ethical imperative. In a world where progress must be continually balanced with preservation, where ingenuity must walk hand-in-hand with moral insight, the legacy of leadership will be judged not by how much energy is harnessed, but by how that energy is used to create a better, more humane world.

As the gentle murmur of the night air enveloped the gathering, the wise storyteller's eyes twinkled in the fading light. The flames of the fire, though reduced in size, continued to burn steadily - mirroring the enduring spark of hope that had been kindled in the hearts of all who listened. It was a reminder that every energy revolution, regardless of its scale or the era in which it occurred, was a tapestry woven from the threads of human endeavour, vision, and the timeless quest for eudaimonia. And in that shared pursuit, spanning from the earliest fire-lit nights to the grand international conferences of today, lay the promise of a future that might yet be redeemed by the wisdom of moral leadership - a future where every act of progress was a promise to our children and the generations yet to come.

In the soft afterglow of that remarkable evening, as listeners began to drift away to their own homes beneath the starry dome, the legacy of Edmund's tale lingered in the quiet spaces between thought and dream. It was a legacy that transcended boundaries and ideologies - a gentle yet powerful call to unify, to lead, and to remember that the true essence of energy was not simply in the power it generated, but in the hope, the aspiration, and the moral responsibility it demanded from every leader. The energy transition, with all its intricate challenges and opportunities, was above all a test of our humanity, a test of whether we could, in the midst of rapid change, still choose to lead with conscience, to forge a legacy built not on transient power, but on enduring care for the world and all who dwell within it.

Thus, when the chill of the night finally overcame the warmth of the receding fire and the small group dispersed into the waiting arms of the dark countryside, each carried with them the seed of a grand idea – a seed that whispered of ancient fires, of industrial revolutions, of modern innovations, and of the high moral calling that bound them all together. The seed was the unyielding belief that true progress was measured not only in energy output or technological wizardry, but in the capacity to enrich human life, to heal the scars of environmental neglect, and to guide the planet towards a future where every decision was an act of stewardship. In that belief lay the promise of moral leadership – an assurance that, despite the occasional misstep of a nation turning its back on the global community, the spirit of cooperation and ethical progress would endure.

And so the narrative of energy and leadership – of flickering fires and sprawling modern grids, of philosophical wisdom and policy debates – continued to unfold, with each new chapter written by the unwavering hands of those who dared to dream of a better, more sustainable future. It was a story that reminded them all that while technology might light up our nights and power our cities, it was our collective moral choices that ultimately determined the brightness of the dawn.

The story that began with a humble flame had, over the ages, illuminated the path from primitive hope to global endeavour. It had shown that every act of leadership – not the leadership of force or mere ambition, but the leadership of conscience and care – carried with it the power to shape destinies. And in the quiet moments of reflection, when all the clamor of modernity settled into a deep, introspective silence, the lesson was as clear as it was enduring: that to lead is to serve, to inspire, and above all, to act as a guardian of both present progress and future promise.

In the end, the essence of energy transitions and moral leadership was one not merely of technological advancements or political maneuvers, but of a deep, abiding commitment to the common good. It was a tale that urged all who heard it to look beyond the transient allure of immediate power – be it the seductive glow of coal-fired engines or the dazzling promises of digital efficiency – and to recognise that true progress was about nurturing a world where every individual, every community, and indeed, every nation, could flourish in harmony with nature. And so it was that, in the fading light of that unforgettable evening, the story of energy, leadership, and the moral imperative to care for our shared home continued to echo – a legacy of hope that promised to guide the way forward, even in the face of daunting challenges and uncertain times.

As each listener returned to their own lives, the lessons of the past mingled with the promise of the future. They carried with them a renewed conviction that, while the journey might be fraught with setbacks and moments of disillusionment, every setback was also an opportunity. An opportunity to reaffirm the belief that leadership grounded in ethical values was the most potent energy of all. A power that, like the ancient flame, could light up the darkest of nights and lead humanity from despair to hope, from fragmentation to unity, and from mere survival to true flourishing.

In that enduring spirit of resilience and moral clarity, the world pressed forward on its long, challenging road – a road where each new dawn held the promise of reconciling innovation with integrity, ambition with accountability, and power with compassion. And it was on this road, paved by the countless acts of leadership that spanned from the earliest fires to the modern-day struggles for sustainability, that the true measure of progress was found - a measure defined not solely by the energy harnessed, but by the enduring light of shared values and the unwavering commitment to leaving behind a legacy worthy of future generations.

Thus, as the stars wheeled overhead and the horizon beckoned with the promise of a new day, the grand narrative of human progress continued its timeless march. A march that, despite occasional falterings - like that fateful withdrawal from the Paris Accord - remained driven by a higher calling, an unyielding dedication to the idea that every spark of energy, every act of leadership, was ultimately a testament to the enduring human spirit. And in that spirit, each soul was invited to play a small yet significant role in the ongoing odyssey toward a world where ethics, innovation, and sustainability united to create a future as bright as the flames that had first ignited human hope so many millennia ago.

6

The Evolution of the Hydrogen Economy

The story of hydrogen is as ancient and boundless as the universe itself - a tale woven into the very fabric of existence that stretches back to the moment when time and space first burst into being following the Big Bang. In those primordial instants, when the cosmos was a seething cauldron of energy and elementary particles, hydrogen emerged as the simplest and most abundant of all elements, destined to become the foundation upon which stars, galaxies, and ultimately the planets were built. In that cosmic dawn, hydrogen was not a mere component; it was the crucible from which the very notion of matter was forged. Yet, despite its omnipresence and central role in the cosmic order, for nearly the entirety of human history, hydrogen remained an enigmatic, unseen substance - a silent witness to the evolution of the universe, largely unrecognised and unable to assert any practical influence over the energy systems of man.

Human civilisation, in its early days, had little cause to be aware of this vast reservoir of potential energy. The elemental force that ignited life's first sparks was fire, and the fuel that sustained it was wood, a resource that grew naturally in abundance. In those ancient times, it was not hydrogen that heated hearths or lit ceremonial torches, but rather a solid, tangible fuel that could be gathered, stored, and ignited by the simplest of methods. As civilisation evolved and technology grew more sophisticated, coal, oil, and gas replaced wood as the dominant energy sources, powering the engines of industrial revolution and fuelling the economic growth of emerging nations. Yet, it was only in our modern age - characterised by advanced scientific research and a burgeoning environmental consciousness - that hydrogen has been rediscovered, not as an inert or elusive substance destined to remain hidden, but as a dynamic, viable energy vector capable of transforming the future of global energy economies.

The journey from a universe saturated with hydrogen to a reality in which economies are built on its potential has been a long, winding path marked by moments of brilliance, periods of stagnation, episodes of setback, and phases of rediscovery. Unlike fossil fuels such as coal or oil, which announce their presence in tangible seams under the earth or in the striking appearance of crude surges atop the ground, hydrogen has always lived in a state of compounded existence. It does not occur freely in its elemental form but is typically bound up with other substances - be it in water, complex hydrocarbons, or myriad organic compounds - and must be painstakingly extracted from these compounds. This inherent elusiveness has required generations of scientists, engineers, and visionaries to solve a host of obstacles, to devise technologies that could separate, compress, transport, and ultimately harness hydrogen in a manner that was efficient and economically viable.

The first flicker of hope in this extensive quest appeared in the later years of the 18th century. It was during this transformative period that the intellectual contributions of figures such as Henry Cavendish and Antoine Lavoisier began to cast light on the mysteries of what would later be known simply as hydrogen. Henry Cavendish - a man whose personality was as reclusive and enigmatic as the substance he studied - was born in 1731 into one of England's most illustrious and wealthy aristocratic families. Despite the expectations placed upon him by his society, Cavendish showed little interest in the trappings of fame or the rituals of high society. Instead, he sought solace in the quiet solitude of his laboratory, a sanctuary where his mind was free to explore the arcane realms of natural philosophy and chemical experimentation. His interactions with the outside world were few and often mediated by written correspondence; he preferred the discreet company of scientific instruments and carefully controlled experiments to the boisterous social scenes of his day.

It was within this environment of disciplined inquiry that Cavendish made one of his most significant, though initially underappreciated, contributions to science. In 1766, through painstaking experiments and meticulous documentation, he became the first to isolate a gas which he termed "inflammable air." In a series of delicate experiments conducted under conditions that would be unthinkable by modern safety standards, he observed that when this invisible gas was ignited, it produced a faint, nearly imperceptible flame - a flame that, remarkably, generated nothing but water on combustion. Although Cavendish did not immediately grasp the full implications of his discovery, his work laid the experimental foundation for the identification of this substance as a new element. Later, inspired by his findings, Antoine Lavoisier would build upon these initial observations, realising that the gas was not merely an oddity, but indeed a fundamental component of water. Lavoisier's rigorous approach to chemical nomenclature and combustion theory eventually led to the realisation that the gas was a key ingredient in the formation of water, and his name for it - hydrogen - was derived from the Greek words "hydro" (water) and "genes" (creator), a poetic nod to its role in birthing life-sustaining compounds.

The legacies of Cavendish and Lavoisier extend far beyond their immediate experimental achievements. Their work instilled in future generations of scientists the importance of precision, persistence, and analytical rigour - a set of virtues that would drive the evolution of energy science and industrial chemistry in the centuries that followed. Cavendish's experiments with hydrogen were remarkable not only for their ingenuity but also for the broader implications they would have on our understanding of matter and energy. His dedication to empirical inquiry and his willingness to delve into the mysteries of a seemingly imperceptible substance set the stage for the eventual dawn of modern chemistry, paving a path that would ultimately lead to the hydrogen economy of the twenty-first century. Had it not been for the careful observations and methodical investigations of men like Cavendish and Lavoisier, the potential of hydrogen as an energy source might still lie dormant, its secrets held tightly within the molecular bonds of water and organic matter.

As the centuries unfurled, hydrogen's journey moved from the quiet ingenuity of laboratory experiments to the expansive ambitions of industrial applications. The first significant foray into the utilisation of hydrogen as a practical fuel came during the late 19th and early 20th centuries, when it found a dramatic application in the realm of airship technology. The vast dirigibles, those majestic leviathans that soared aloft on seas of blue sky, were designed with enormous gasbags filled with hydrogen. Their elegant, elongated forms seemed to glide effortlessly across continents, capturing the collective imagination of an era that was both enthralled by the promise of modern engineering and yet haunted by the spectre of disaster. For many, hydrogen symbolised not only technological progress and the allure of human ingenuity, but also the inherent risks that come with harnessing a substance of such volatile energy.

In the early decades of airship travel, hydrogen-powered balloons and dirigibles symbolised the pinnacle of aeronautical engineering. Entire economies invested in the technologies required to build these majestic vessels, with substantial financial, technological, and human resource allocations directed toward mastering the challenges of hydrogen containment, buoyancy control, and aerodynamics. Advanced techniques were developed to handle the delicate balance required when filling enormous envelopes with a gas that, while offering unparalleled lift due to its low molecular weight, was prone to leakage and explosive reactivity under certain conditions. The promise of hydrogen in these early applications, however, was forever tarnished by a catastrophe that would echo throughout the annals of history. The infamous Hindenburg disaster of 1937, in which a hydrogen-filled airship ended in a calamitous inferno above New Jersey, served as a harrowing reminder of the dangers inherent in managing this volatile element. The tragedy was seared into public consciousness, and for decades afterward, hydrogen was viewed less as an emblem of progress and more as a perilous liability.

Despite this setback, the shadow of hydrogen's potential loomed large over the scientific and industrial communities. Even as the promise of aerial travel succumbed to caution and fear, another frontier beckoned - a boundary that lay not in the skies above Earth, but beyond our planet's atmosphere itself. In the mid-20th century, as the world embarked on the great endeavour of space exploration, humanity revisited the chemical properties of hydrogen. The very qualities that had once made it a risky choice for civilian transport now rendered it an indispensable resource for space travel. Its extremely low density and high energy yield when combined with liquid oxygen made it an ideal candidate for rocket propulsion, and hydrogen-fired engines soon became the driving force behind some of the most ambitious space missions in history. The Saturn V rocket, a colossal achievement of engineering, harnessed the power of hydrogen combustion to escape Earth's gravitational pull and carry astronauts safely to the moon - a symbolic triumph that underscored hydrogen's remarkable ability to be controlled and utilised with extraordinary precision in conditions where human ingenuity had pushed the boundaries of what was thought possible.

The successful deployment of hydrogen as a rocket fuel opened new avenues of thought. If this lightest of elements could be effectively managed to propel massive spacecraft into the void of space, it stood as a testament to the potential for hydrogen to revolutionise terrestrial energy systems. This realisation came at a time when the world was beginning to confront the limitations of reliance on fossil fuels. The energy crises of the 1970s, marked by staggering oil shocks and an increasing awareness of environmental degradation, rekindled interest in hydrogen as a means to secure energy independence and reduce the damaging emissions associated with traditional fossil fuel consumption. Visionaries and policymakers began to debate whether hydrogen might offer a cleaner, more sustainable alternative - a prospect that promised not only to alleviate the immediate pressures of energy scarcity but also to pave the way for a long-term transition towards environmental stewardship.

The ambition to harness hydrogen as an alternative energy source rapidly attracted the attention of governments, research institutions, and industrial stakeholders around the world. Significant investments flowed into research on advanced electrolysis techniques, novel catalysts, and the development of fuel cell technologies capable of converting the energy stored in hydrogen directly into electricity with minimal environmental impact. Cutting-edge research began exploring innovative methods of producing green hydrogen, which is generated through the electrolysis of water powered by renewable energy sources such as wind, solar, and tidal systems. The technology required both substantial capital investment and a robust interdisciplinary approach combining materials science, chemical engineering, and systems design. State-of-the-art electrolyser systems, once considered experimental, gradually transitioned from laboratories to pilot projects and demonstration plants, each iteration driven by the urgent need to reduce global reliance on carbon-intensive fuels.

The technological journey to a fully operational hydrogen economy is a story of relentless experimentation and iterative progress. Researchers have since sought to overcome the fundamental challenges associated with hydrogen production and storage. One of the principal hurdles is its method of extraction. While the most common technique - steam methane reforming - is currently widely used for hydrogen production, it relies heavily on fossil fuels and emits significant amounts of carbon dioxide. For hydrogen to truly become a clean energy carrier, the focus must shift toward green hydrogen, produced by the electrolysis of water using renewable energy. In addition, innovative approaches in thermochemical cycles, biological production methods, and even solar-driven electrolysis have been the subjects of intense investigation. Each of these technologies requires not only groundbreaking scientific research but also the scaling up of production facilities, the development of more efficient systems, and the integration of global supply chains capable of handling large-scale hydrogen production and distribution.

One of the remarkable facets of this transformation is the intricate network of investments in infrastructure and research that has been mobilised over the last few decades. Governments across Europe, Asia, and North America have committed billions of pounds, euros, and dollars to fostering a hydrogen economy that aligns with their environmental and energy security goals. In the European Union, for instance, hydrogen has been declared a cornerstone of the Green Deal, a sweeping initiative to render the continent carbon-neutral by mid-century. This ambitious strategy involves financing innovative research projects, constructing Hydrogen valleys where renewable energy and hydrogen production are intricately integrated, and modernising the transport and energy grid infrastructure to accommodate hydrogen's unique characteristics. Concurrently, nations endowed with vast renewable energy resources have begun to view hydrogen not only as an energy carrier for domestic consumption but also as a potential export commodity that could transform their economies. Australia, blessed with expansive solar and wind resources, is in the process of developing itself into one of the world's leading suppliers of green hydrogen, with significant investments directed towards creating the infrastructure necessary to produce, store, and ship hydrogen to markets across Asia and beyond.

While the practical applications of hydrogen as a fuel have been widely publicised in the context of space exploration and even aviation, its true renaissance is currently unfolding within the industrial sector. As the realities of climate change have become inescapable, a pressing imperative has emerged to decarbonise the most energy-intensive and intransigent sectors of the modern economy - industries such as steel production, cement manufacturing, and chemical processing, which have long relied on fossil fuels to generate the high temperatures and sustained reactions required for production. In these sectors, the substitution of conventional fossil fuels with hydrogen is not merely a matter of environmental preference; it is emerging as a critical strategy for reshaping the industrial landscape in a way that aligns with global commitments to sustainability. Hydrogen, with its unique capacity to supply both high-quality heat and oxygen-free environments for chemical reactions, has been identified as one of the very few alternatives capable of replacing the entrenched use of coal and gas in these heavy industries. The vision is bold: to transition from a carbon-intensive industrial paradigm to one in which hydrogen runs the furnaces of steel mills, powers the kilns of cement factories, and feeds the chemical reactions underpinning countless products that modern society relies upon.

Yet, despite the immense promise of hydrogen as a catalyst for industrial transformation, scaling up such systems is fraught with technological challenges that demand interdisciplinary cooperation and sustained financial commitment. For instance, the transport of hydrogen from production sites to industrial users is not a trivial task. The element's propensity to leak - owing to its tiny molecular size - necessitates the development of specialised transport pipelines and storage containers composed of materials resistant to hydrogen embrittlement. Engineers and materials scientists have spent decades investigating novel alloys and composite materials capable of resisting these corrosive effects, but widespread implementation remains one of the major areas where further investment and research are critically required. Additionally, compressing hydrogen for storage or pipeline transit demands energy-intensive processes, and finding ways to optimise these processes is essential to ensuring that the overall energy balance remains favourable when hydrogen is compared to more conventional fuels.

The investments required to establish a robust hydrogen economy extend not only to the development of new technologies but also to the reconfiguration of existing energy infrastructures. In a world long dominated by networks built for oil and gas, the transition to a hydrogen-powered future will require a complete rewiring of energy grids, refuelling systems, and even safety protocols that have been honed over centuries to manage different kinds of fuels. Governments and private stakeholders are now confronted with the need to retrofit aging infrastructures, construct entirely new networks of pipelines and storage facilities, and develop monitoring systems that can oversee the safe handling of hydrogen at every stage of the supply chain. This is not a transformation that can be achieved overnight – it is a gradual process that will necessitate the deployment of substantial public and private capital, alongside regulatory frameworks that encourage innovation while protecting public safety and the environment.

The evolution of hydrogen technology is underpinned by a series of fascinating, interlocking innovations. Among these is the development of fuel cell technology, first conceptualised in the 19th century but only in recent decades refined to the point of commercial viability. A fuel cell converts the chemical energy stored in hydrogen into direct electrical energy through an electrochemical process, bypassing the need for combustion and thus significantly reducing emissions. This technology is being applied across a diverse range of sectors, from powering remote telecommunications equipment and emergency backup systems to potentially providing distributed energy solutions for residential and commercial buildings. The inherent efficiency and scalability of fuel cells make them a promising bridge technology in the broader energy transition.

At the laboratory and pilot-scale levels, advanced materials play a crucial role in the efficiency of hydrogen-based systems. Researchers have been exploring nanostructured catalysts, often comprised of platinum-group metals or emerging alternatives, which facilitate the critical reactions in both electrolyser and fuel cell systems. The goal is to reduce the reliance on scarce, expensive catalysts by identifying materials that are abundant yet equally efficient in promoting hydrogen production and energy conversion. This line of research not only promises to make green hydrogen production more cost-effective but also holds the potential to drive down the overall capital investments required for large-scale hydrogen infrastructure. Many academic institutions and research organisations around the globe are now engaged in collaborative projects that bridge the gap between fundamental scientific research and applied technological development, working in tandem with industry leaders to commercialise breakthrough innovations.

The role of visionary leadership in advancing the hydrogen economy cannot be understated. It was, after all, the curiosity and determination of early figures like Henry Cavendish and Antoine Lavoisier that first unlocked the mysteries of hydrogen, setting an example for generations of scientists and engineers to follow. Cavendish's delicate experiments, conducted in an era when the scientific method was still in its formative stages, laid bare the elemental properties of hydrogen long before society had any notion of its potential industrial applications. His isolated pursuit of knowledge, often conducted in the quiet seclusion of his laboratory away from the distractions of aristocratic life, is a testament to the power of individual curiosity to drive forward the boundaries of human understanding. Similarly, Lavoisier's rigorous reformation of chemical nomenclature and his insistence on precision in experimental design not only clarified the nature of hydrogen but also established a framework for modern scientific inquiry that endures to this day.

In recognising these pioneering contributions, modern advocates of the hydrogen economy frequently draw parallels between the challenges faced by early chemists and the obstacles confronting contemporary researchers. The transition to a hydrogen-based energy system, much like the early experiments that sought to reveal its secrets, requires perseverance, a willingness to embrace complex technical challenges, and the coordination of immense financial and intellectual resources. In a sense, the legacy of Cavendish and Lavoisier lives on in every modern experiment, every multi-million-pound investment in electrolysers and fuel cells, and every government policy that aims to create a sustainable, hydrogen-fuelled future for generations to come.

The decades that followed the early revelations about hydrogen saw a series of intermittent advances that punctuated periods of both hope and scepticism. During the interwar years and the immediate post-war era, industrial progress often hinged on short-term gains from established fossil fuel sources, and hydrogen was relegated to the realm of theoretical promise rather than practical application. However, as global awareness of environmental degradation and resource scarcity grew, a renewed sense of urgency began to permeate political and scientific discussions. Policymakers became increasingly aware that the future of energy would not be secured by clinging to finite resources but by embracing the renewable, inexhaustible potential of alternatives such as hydrogen. This realisation spurred a wave of international collaborations and public-private partnerships aimed at overcoming the fundamental obstacles to hydrogen utilisation.

One vivid strand of this renewed interest was its application in sectors that had long resisted modernisation through conventional electrification. Industrial plants that produced steel, chemicals, and cement - industries notorious for their heavy carbon footprints - began to reimagine their processes in ways that could incorporate hydrogen as both a fuel and a chemical feedstock. For example, in steel production, hydrogen can be employed as a reducing agent in processes traditionally dominated by coke and coal. In doing so, it not only facilitates the extraction of iron from ore but also substantially lowers the associated carbon emissions. The process, while technically challenging, offers a tantalising glimpse of how hydrogen could reshape fundamental industrial techniques that have changed little in over a century.

Emerging pilot projects and demonstration plants around the world have provided valuable insights into the practicalities of this industrial revitalisation. Engineers and scientists, working on prototypes and small-scale models, have demonstrated that the use of hydrogen in high-temperature industrial processes can achieve performance metrics comparable to traditional fuels, yet without the environmental toll. These projects often require close cooperation between academics, industrial engineers, financial institutions, and government agencies, all of whom contribute resources, expertise, and capital. Their collaborative efforts illustrate that the future of hydrogen is not the result of any single breakthrough but rather a gradual, systemic evolution involving incremental improvements, regulatory reforms, and a reimagining of entire industrial ecosystems.

The scale of investment required to bring the hydrogen economy into full bloom is enormous, yet many governments and private companies appear undaunted. In recent years, a host of initiatives have been launched to support both the supply side and the demand side of hydrogen technology. Across Europe, multi-billion-pound investment strategies have been unveiled, encompassing projects that range from the construction of giga-scale electrolyser facilities to the development of long-distance hydrogen pipelines that will connect renewable energy sources with industrial hubs. In Asia, nations with robust manufacturing sectors and dense urban populations have initiated pilot programmes designed to integrate hydrogen fuel cells into public transportation networks, energy grids, and even residential heating systems. In North America, research and development clusters have emerged around major research universities and innovation centres where cutting-edge experiments in hydrogen storage, composite materials, and catalytic converter technologies are rapidly advancing the state of the art.

The realisation of a hydrogen economy is inextricably linked to advancements in digital technologies as well. The integration of artificial intelligence, machine learning, and big data analytics into hydrogen production and distribution systems is poised to revolutionise how these complex networks are managed. Real-time monitoring of hydrogen flow, pressure, and quality can enhance safety protocols and optimise energy efficiency across the entire supply chain. Furthermore, automated control systems, supported by robust algorithms, are being developed to predict and adjust operational parameters in response to dynamic demand fluctuations, thereby ensuring that energy production remains both cost-effective and sustainable. These technological innovations are critical to overcoming the practical challenges of scaling hydrogen infrastructure, as they not only improve performance and safety but also play a pivotal role in reducing operational costs - a key factor given the high capital expenditure associated with transitioning from fossil fuels to hydrogen.

Despite the many advances and encouraging pilot projects, the path towards a widespread hydrogen economy is not free of obstacles. For one, the conversion of our current energy systems – characterised by well-established networks for electricity, oil, and gas – into ones that can support hydrogen on a mass scale requires a fundamental shift in both policy and infrastructure. Retrofitting existing pipelines, building new hydrogen refuelling stations, and reforming safety standards are tasks that demand years of planning, coordination, and investment. In addition, public perception and acceptance remain significant challenges; the memory of historical disasters, coupled with the inherent technical complexities of hydrogen technology, mean that widespread adoption must be accompanied by clear communication and education. Stakeholders from various sectors are actively engaged in dialogue to address these issues, forging partnerships across borders and industries in the shared pursuit of a cleaner, more sustainable energy future.

It is a journey fraught with both technical challenges and human ambition – a modern epic that is unfolding in research laboratories, industrial plants, and policy chambers around the world. As each new breakthrough emerges, as each pilot project meets its milestones, the promise of a hydrogen economy grows ever more tangible, even as its realisation remains contingent on sustained investment and unwavering commitment to innovation. The lessons of history – whether it be the patient, meticulous experiments of Cavendish or the transformative insights of Lavoisier – remind us that the pursuit of knowledge and the transformation of society are processes that demand time, resilience, and imagination.

Today, the advanced scientific tools at our disposal would have been unimaginable to the early chemists who grappled with the nature of hydrogen. Mass spectrometry, high-performance computing, and quantum mechanical modelling now allow researchers to predict and manipulate molecular interactions with astonishing precision. These developments not only accelerate the discovery of more efficient catalysts and improved storage materials but also help refine the operational parameters of industrial-scale hydrogen production. For instance, novel materials such as metal-organic frameworks and advanced carbon nanostructures are being investigated for their ability to adsorb and store hydrogen at high densities under ambient conditions. These technological innovations, which lie at the intersection of chemistry, physics, and materials science, are paving the way for the next generation of hydrogen systems that combine efficiency with cost-effectiveness - a crucial convergence if hydrogen is to become the backbone of our future energy infrastructure.

The transformation towards a hydrogen-based economy is not merely a technological challenge; it is a societal endeavour that will redefine economic priorities, environmental responsibilities, and global energy security. If we are to navigate this path successfully, we must embrace both the potential and the inherent challenges of hydrogen, recognising that its full realisation is a long-term commitment that transcends narrow political cycles or fleeting economic trends. International cooperation, combined with visionary investments in research and infrastructure, will forge the road ahead - a road that promises cleaner air, more resilient energy systems, and a more sustainable coexistence with the planet that sustains us.

In reflecting upon the remarkable journey of hydrogen - from its cosmic origins to its emerging role in our modern energy landscape - one cannot help but feel a sense of wonder at the inherent possibilities that nature offers. The lightest and most abundant element in all creation, once hidden in the minutiae of atomic structure, now stands ready to underpin a transformative economic revolution. The pursuit of a hydrogen economy is not a mere technical challenge; it is a quest to harmonise human civilisation with the deep, underlying forces that have shaped our universe since time immemorial. It is an endeavour that echoes with the same spirit of exploration and discovery that guided early experimentalists like Henry Cavendish and Antoine Lavoisier – men who, in their quiet laboratories and amidst the rigours of scientific inquiry, laid the cornerstone for a future that now appears not remote, but imminently achievable.

As we look to the horizon of the twenty-first century and beyond, the role of hydrogen is set to expand further into every facet of human endeavour. From the industries that churn out the materials of modern life to the transport networks that connect our cities, from the energy grids that power our homes to the space missions that push the boundaries of our knowledge, hydrogen's fingerprints are beginning to appear more frequently than ever before. Each step forward in the adoption of hydrogen-based technologies is a testament to the enduring legacy of those who dared to question the conventional and to dream of a future where the fundamental building blocks of the cosmos could be harnessed for the betterment of humankind.

There is no single moment that will define the triumph of the hydrogen economy; rather, it is a mosaic of countless incremental advances, each building upon the achievements of previous generations. The investments required to reengineer our infrastructure, optimise production processes, and integrate cutting-edge digital technologies are substantial, yet they pale in comparison to the long-term benefits of a sustainable, resilient, and environmentally responsible energy ecosystem. As nations commit to ambitious targets for carbon reduction and renewable energy penetration, hydrogen is rapidly emerging as a critical partner in this global transformation – a partner that promises to bridge the gaps where other technologies fall short.

In the face of these challenges, the spirit of innovation that characterised the work of early pioneers continues to shine. Researchers across the globe, armed with modern equipment and driven by the urgency of climate change, are exploring new paradigms for energy storage and transport that rely on hydrogen's unique properties. Moreover, the financial commitments of governments and industries, inspired by the possibility of a radically improved energy future, keep growing stronger year after year. These investments, both public and private, are not simply bets on a new technology but affirmations of the collective belief that the future of energy lies in breaking down old paradigms and building anew – a future in which hydrogen is not merely an alternative, but a linchpin of our global energy matrix.

In this unfolding saga, every laboratory experiment, every industrial pilot project, every policy initiative, and every stroke of innovative brilliance contributes a vital chapter. The deep scientific discoveries of the 18th century have matured into technological innovations that promise to drive the decarbonisation of entire economic sectors. As we stand at this critical juncture, the imperative is clear: we must look to the future with the same courage, curiosity, and commitment that once led Henry Cavendish to isolate "inflammable air" in his secluded laboratory. It is this same spirit that will guide us through the complex, multifaceted journey of reimagining our energy systems for a sustainable tomorrow.

Looking back over the centuries, it becomes evident that the evolution of hydrogen - like all great journeys - is one of both continuity and transformation. The pioneering work of figures such as Cavendish and Lavoisier laid the early conceptual groundwork, demonstrating that even the most unassuming substances can harbour extraordinary potential. Their discoveries, conducted in a time when scientific experimentation was both dangerous and revolutionary, now resonate with a modern urgency to reshape our technological futures. Today, the re-emergence of hydrogen as a cornerstone element of energy strategy is not simply a revisitation of historical insights; it is an affirmation that the best ideas often endure, evolving with each generation as technology sheds new light on age-old mysteries.

The integration of hydrogen into the global energy landscape will require considerable ingenuity - a willingness to invest not only in the physical infrastructure of pipes, plants, and pipelines, but also in the intangible assets of knowledge, research, and international cooperation. This grand transformation, which is as much a cultural and political endeavour as it is a technical one, holds the promise of delivering the clean, efficient, and resilient energy systems that modern society so desperately needs. It is a call to embrace complexity and to invest in a future where, much like the quiet, persistent work of early chemists, innovation is gradually and inexorably turned into a force for the common good.

As the narrative of hydrogen continues to unfurl, intertwining with the unfolding drama of climate change and sustainable development, we are reminded that our choices today will echo through the centuries. Just as the discovery of fire once propelled humanity into a new era of civilisation and the steam engine heralded the industrial revolution, the widescale adoption of hydrogen technology may be the catalyst for yet another transformation – one that promises to harmonise our industrial might with the imperatives of environmental stewardship. It is in this context that every investment, every research breakthrough, and every policy reform aimed at advancing hydrogen technology must be seen as an investment in the collective future of humanity.

In the end, the evolution of hydrogen encapsulates a microcosm of the human experience – a journey from obscurity to prominence, from theoretical potential to practical application, from the realm of experimental laboratories to the heart of global industry. It is a journey marked by determination, intellectual bravery, and a steadfast belief in the capacity of human ingenuity to overcome even the most daunting challenges. As we write the next chapters in this epic tale, the lessons of the past provide both guidance and inspiration. The contributions of Henry Cavendish and Antoine Lavoisier remind us that great discoveries often begin with small, deliberate steps taken in the quiet pursuit of knowledge. Their legacy is woven into the fabric of the modern hydrogen revolution, a testament to the enduring power of curiosity and the transformative impact of dedicated scientific endeavour.

The road ahead is long and punctuated by significant obstacles, but it is also brimming with promise. With every passing year, as technological advancements continue to lower production costs and improve the efficiency of hydrogen systems, the notion of a complete energy transformation grows less fanciful and more tangible. We find ourselves at a pivotal moment in human history, where the convergence of environmental imperatives, technological breakthroughs, and significant financial commitments is poised to deliver a truly sustainable energy future. The hydrogen economy, informed both by centuries-old wisdom and by modern scientific advances, stands ready to play a central role in steering our global society toward a cleaner, more resilient tomorrow.

In summary, the journey of hydrogen - from its glittering cosmic origins to its modern resurgence as a key component of our sustainable future - is a narrative of innovation, persistence, and transformative potential. It is a story that spans the eons, from the humble experiments of Henry Cavendish in his secluded laboratory to the sprawling infrastructure projects funded by governments and industries around the world today. As we continue to invest in research, develop new technologies, and commit to sweeping changes in our energy systems, the legacy of hydrogen offers a beacon of hope. It tells us that even the simplest elements can carry the promise of extraordinary change, provided we have the courage to embrace their potential. And so, as we stride forward into the uncertain future of the 21st century, it is with a deep sense of purpose, informed by the past and inspired by the possibilities of tomorrow, that we commit to the pursuit of a hydrogen economy - a task as monumental as it is necessary, a challenge that, if met, may very well define the next great chapter in the history of human civilisation.

Thus, the age-old story of hydrogen, interlaced with threads of scientific brilliance and monumental investments, continues to evolve, promising a future where the silent force once concealed in the vastness of space emerges as the vibrant engine that powers our world. There remains much work to be done, much infrastructure to be built and refined, and many technical challenges to overcome. Yet, in this pursuit, there is a certain timeless continuity - a modern echo of the enduring spirit of discovery that first set human knowledge ablaze with the illumination of fire and later powered entire industries to unprecedented heights. In the quest to harness hydrogen as a clean, sustainable energy source, we stand at the threshold of a new era, one that is as promising as it is challenging, as intricate as it is revolutionary. And in this grand endeavour, the contributions of those who came before us - of Henry Cavendish with his meticulous experiments and Antoine Lavoisier with his profound insights - remain a guiding light, reminding us that the pursuit of knowledge, when combined with the will to act, can change the world.

7

Jevons' Paradox - The Future of AI and Computing

In 1865, an astute British economist by the name of William Stanley Jevons observed a phenomenon that would eventually be encapsulated in what we now call Jevons' Paradox. At a time when the advances in steam engine technology were heralding the dawn of the industrial age, Jevons noted with no small measure of surprise that as these engines became increasingly efficient in their use of coal, the overall consumption of coal did not decline as one might intuitively expect. Instead, the increased efficiency led to a reduction in the cost of energy, which in turn spurred a proliferation of coal-dependent industries. The resulting economic dynamism meant that far more coal was being used than had been before, thus establishing a cycle of ever-growing consumption - a cycle that remains as relevant in today's technologically saturated world as it was in the nineteenth century.

In an era dominated by artificial intelligence, omnipresent data centres, and an insatiable hunger for computation, the parallels with steam power are striking indeed. Modern computational devices, from humble microprocessors in smartphones to the sprawling server farms that power cloud computing, all underscore a singular truth: technological efficiency often becomes a double-edged sword. Every new advance in artificial intelligence hardware and software seems initially to promise lower operational costs and a reduction in resource use; yet, as history has demonstrated, this very efficiency ignites a cascade of additional demand. Just as the steam engine's increased efficiency paved the way for more industries to adopt coal as a power source, leading to an explosion in demand, today's more powerful processors and sophisticated AI algorithms only serve to reinforce an ever-spiralling appetite for computational power.

This phenomenon is not confined to a single industry but is instead reflective of a broader economic reality. The modern world – with its reliance on search engines that can process vast repositories of information in an instant, financial markets operating at the speed of thought, and cloud storage solutions underpinning everything from social media to scientific research – lives in a grand state of computational dependency. Data centres, those modern-day factories of digital information, stand as a testament to this evolution. In 2023, estimates indicated that global data centres consumed somewhere between 240 and 340 terawatt-hours of electricity – an amount that represented roughly one to one and a third per cent of worldwide electricity demand. Projections suggest that by 2030, this energy consumption could potentially double or even triple in response to the relentless push for more advanced artificial intelligence, machine learning, and cloud computing technologies.

The economic implications of this transformation are far-reaching. Efficiency gains in data processing, while admirable in their own right, are frequently outpaced by the scale and velocity of new applications demanding ever more power. When one examines the historical continuum of energy transitions, the pattern is unmistakable. The Industrial Revolution was powered by coal, the motorisation of the twentieth century was driven by oil, and now, we witness a world where electricity fuels an increasingly digital economy. However, the speed with which we are now traversing these transitions is unprecedented. Artificial intelligence and data-driven applications are experiencing exponential growth, challenging the very notion that increases in efficiency can outstrip corresponding rises in consumption. The challenge we face today is not merely technical; it is deeply economic and ecological as well.

To understand the full ramifications of this paradox, one must delve into the historical patterns that have accompanied major shifts in energy consumption. In the nineteenth century, the invention of more efficient steam engines initially promised to reduce the consumption of coal. Yet, as industries discovered that the lower cost of energy could significantly enhance their production capacities, the total consumption only increased. This is the crux of Jevons' argument, one that would be echoed in subsequent centuries with different energy sources. Take, for instance, the rise of oil in the twentieth century. Oil did not replace coal because coal became inherently inefficient; rather, oil offered distinct advantages in terms of energy density and the flexibility it provided in powering emerging industries such as the automotive and aviation sectors. The lesson is clear: technological improvements in efficiency, though beneficial in a narrow sense, end up driving broader consumption when they stimulate new uses and applications.

Similarly, today we witness a comparable scenario in the realm of digital computation and artificial intelligence. Innovations in semiconductor manufacturing, most famously encapsulated in Moore's Law, once promised that transistor counts would double approximately every two years, leading to steadily more powerful processors and concomitant improvements in energy efficiency. This steady march of progress allowed for incremental enhancements that, when aggregated, yielded significant performance boosts without a corresponding increase in power usage. However, the rise of artificial intelligence has markedly disrupted this predictable pattern. Modern AI systems, such as the GPT series of language models, are computational behemoths, requiring orders of magnitude more power than traditional software applications. For example, the training of GPT-3 alone is estimated to have consumed somewhere around 1.3 gigawatt-hours of electricity – a figure that dwarfs the annual consumption of over a hundred typical U.S. households. Even the seemingly trivial individual queries sent to ChatGPT, when considered en masse, constitute a massive aggregation of power usage. Some estimates even suggest that each such interaction uses roughly ten times the energy of a standard Google search, highlighting a stark irony: as our technology becomes more refined and capable, its energy appetite grows in lockstep.

The situation is exacerbated as data centres scramble to keep pace with the escalating power demands of artificial intelligence. The emergence of hyperscale facilities, operated by tech giants like Google, Amazon, and Microsoft, is a testament to the scale of the challenge. These facilities, sprawling over hundreds of thousands of square metres, are filled with countless racks of high-performance GPUs and specialised processors, all of which require constant cooling and an uninterrupted supply of electricity. In response to such demands, the industry has sought out innovative solutions aimed at maximising energy efficiency in a bid to mitigate some of the environmental impact. For instance, advancements such as NVIDIA's Blackwell architecture represent state-of-the-art efforts to improve efficiency by 40 to 50 per cent, relative to previous iterations. Nonetheless, under the logic of Jevons' Paradox, these gains in efficiency are unlikely to lead to a reduction in overall consumption. Instead, they are likely to fuel further expansion in the deployment of artificial intelligence across nearly every conceivable aspect of society.

This relentless drive for greater computational power is reshaping not just the technical landscape, but the very geography of economic activity as well. Historically, industrial hubs in the nineteenth century sprang up around coal mines, where the supply of raw energy was both plentiful and cheap. Today, we witness analogous phenomena in the clustering of data centres and digital infrastructure around regions that boast reliable and cost-effective power. Regions such as Virginia in the United States, Ireland in Europe, and Singapore in Asia have risen as critical hubs for global data centre operations. In these locales, the pressure on local electrical grids is sometimes so intense that governments have been forced to impose moratoriums or outright bans on the construction of new facilities. Dublin, for example, has experienced such a confluence of rapid data centre expansion that concerns over national energy stability have led to a temporary halt on further development. Similarly, Singapore, with its naturally limited land area and constrained power supply, enacted a pause on new data centre projects in 2019 to avoid jeopardising its energy infrastructure.

Yet, as local grids strain under the pressure of extant demand, the global appetite for artificial intelligence continues to grow unabated. One potential avenue for alleviating the power crunch is the burgeoning field of edge computing. This approach seeks to decentralise computational tasks by locating them closer to the user, rather than relying exclusively on massive centralised data centres. Edge computing promises to reduce latency and improve overall efficiency by dispersing the computational load over a wide network of smaller, geographically distributed nodes. However, even this innovation adheres to the principle of Jevons' Paradox. With more efficient processing happening at the periphery of the network, developers are encouraged to create even more applications that exploit these gains, ultimately leading to further increases in overall energy consumption.

Looking back at historical energy transitions, an additional analogy emerges when one considers the shift from coal to oil in the twentieth century. Oil, with its high energy density and versatility, did not conquer the energy market by rendering coal obsolete solely through efficiency improvements; instead, oil provided qualitatively different advantages - such as ease of storage and transport - that allowed it to fuel a new generation of industrial and societal transformations. Today, the transition facing modern society is not about abandoning electricity - for our digital economy is inextricably linked to it - but about rethinking how that electricity is generated, distributed, and consumed in the context of burgeoning artificial intelligence. Renewable energy sources, nuclear power stations, and sophisticated grid management systems are all being investigated as potential panaceas to the challenge of meeting AI's voracious energy demands. However, it remains an open question whether these greener sources can keep pace with the exponential growth in consumption that appears to be an inherent consequence of ever-increasing computational efficiency.

The environmental ramifications of this trend are profound and cannot be understated. Artificial intelligence offers many promising applications aimed at optimising energy use and combating climate change, such as through the efficient management of power grids and the optimisation of industrial processes. At the same time, however, the very tools designed to combat environmental degradation are themselves significant contributors to carbon emissions. The irony is palpable: in our efforts to combat climate change with the power of AI, we unwittingly drive the demand for energy that in turn exacerbates environmental pressures. The challenge, then, lies in reconciling the dual imperatives of technological progress and environmental stewardship.

This leads us to a pivotal and challenging question: in the face of Jevons' Paradox, can artificial intelligence ever be truly sustainable? The answer may well depend on a multifaceted strategy that incorporates not only further technological breakthroughs but also robust policy interventions and a radical rethinking of how AI infrastructure is conceptualised. It is increasingly clear that if we are to navigate the turbulent waters of future energy demand, we must place energy efficiency at the heart of our planning rather than considering it an afterthought. This may involve rethinking optimal data centre locations, integrating novel technologies such as carbon capture and storage with high-emission power sources, and implementing policies designed to encourage sustainable energy use in both the public and private sectors.

Parallel to these discussions about classical computation and energy consumption is the emerging field of quantum computing, which promises to rewrite many of the rules that have long governed the technological landscape. Quantum computing is predicated on an entirely different set of principles from those that underpin classical computing. Rather than relying on the binary encoding of information using ones and zeros, quantum systems exploit the phenomena of superposition and entanglement. In a quantum computer, qubits can exist in multiple states simultaneously, which theoretically allows these devices to process a vast number of possibilities in parallel. This radical departure from traditional computation means that, for certain types of problems, quantum machines could achieve solutions in mere seconds - solutions that would take classical systems millennia to compute.

The economic implications of quantum computing, if it reaches widespread commercial viability, are staggering. At its core, the promise of quantum technology lies in its potential to dramatically reduce the energy requirements of computation by solving complex problems more directly and more efficiently than classical processors ever could. Major technology firms, including Google, IBM, and a host of ambitious startups like IonQ, are investing vast resources into scaling quantum technology so that it can be brought into practical, real-world use. The promise of a quantum revolution holds out the possibility of breaking free from the self-reinforcing cycle identified by Jevons, potentially curbing the insatiable energy demands of artificial intelligence and ushering in an era in which computational tasks are accomplished with unprecedented efficiency.

Yet, it would be an oversimplification to regard quantum computing solely as a panacea for the energy problems associated with AI. Although the theoretical advantages are immense, the field of quantum computing is still in its nascent stages. Many significant technical challenges remain before it can be deployed on a scale that would make a tangible impact on global energy consumption patterns. The difficulty of maintaining quantum coherence, mitigating errors, and scaling up the number of qubits are all issues that researchers continue to grapple with. Moreover, the economic investments required to transition from classical to quantum computing infrastructure are likely to be enormous. Policymakers, industry leaders, and academic researchers must therefore engage in a nuanced dialogue about the role of quantum computing – not only as a potential solution to computational inefficiencies but also as a transformative technology with its own set of economic, environmental, ethical, and security implications.

The ethical dimensions of quantum computing, in particular, deserve careful scrutiny. The disruptive potential of quantum technologies extends far beyond energy efficiency and computational speed. One of the most immediate concerns is the impact on current cybersecurity systems. Quantum computers, when fully developed, could break many of the cryptographic protocols that presently secure our financial systems, government communications, and personal data. This prospect necessitates a complete rethinking of encryption standards, as the very security of information infrastructure may face fundamental vulnerabilities in a quantum future.

Here, the paradox of progress makes itself doubly apparent: in our relentless pursuit of technological supremacy and efficiency, we may inadvertently compromise the very systems that underpin our social and economic well-being.

In broader economic terms, the diffusion of quantum computing could have transformative effects on industries as varied as finance, logistics, healthcare, and beyond. Financial institutions might leverage quantum algorithms to optimise investment portfolios, manage risk more effectively, or even simulate complex market dynamics with a level of precision that is unattainable today. Similarly, a point that my son and I discussed often, in healthcare, quantum computing could accelerate the process of drug discovery, model biological systems at a molecular level, and ultimately contribute to breakthroughs in our understanding of diseases and medicines. Each of these applications, while promising, also carries with it the potential for unforeseen economic disruptions. The winners of the next technological revolution may well be those who are best able to manage the transition from a classical to a quantum paradigm, navigating both the opportunities and the attendant challenges with foresight and responsibility.

It is also imperative to consider the geopolitical ramifications of these technological advances. Nations that control or have ready access to abundant, competitively priced energy resources are likely to find themselves in a favourable position in the global competition for data centre supremacy and, eventually, quantum computing leadership. Countries such as Norway, Canada, and the United Arab Emirates, endowed with rich reserves of renewable energy and a commitment to sustainable development, are positioning themselves as the new powerhouses of digital infrastructure. This reconfiguration of global power dynamics is not simply a matter of economic competitiveness - it intersects with issues of national security, environmental responsibility, and public policy. Countries grappling with unstable power grids and constrained energy resources face an existential dilemma: should they prioritise the development of AI and digital infrastructure, or should they conserve energy for more direct human needs? The tension between economic growth, energy security, and environmental stewardship is increasingly shaping international relations, and it will likely become a defining element of global strategy in the years ahead.

Returning to the heart of the matter, the challenge imposed by Jevons' Paradox is one that touches both economic theory and practical policy-making. On the one hand, the paradox exposes a fundamental tension in the way that efficiency gains are absorbed by the wider economy. On the other hand, it raises difficult questions about whether technological advances can ever truly outpace their own appetite for energy. The historical record suggests that every time a new era of technology emerges - from steam power to oil to electricity - total consumption tends to rise. In our current digital epoch, this trend appears no less inescapable, even as we develop increasingly sophisticated means of managing and optimising energy usage.

In contemplating the future of artificial intelligence and quantum computing, one must recognise that the ultimate sustainable path forward may lie at the intersection of several disparate strategies. Technological breakthroughs in semiconductor manufacturing and quantum devices might be complemented by stringent regulatory measures aimed at enforcing energy efficiency standards. Economic incentives, such as tax credits for the development of green technology or public investments in renewable infrastructure, may also play a crucial role in steering the industry towards a more sustainable future. Furthermore, international cooperation will be vital, as energy and digital infrastructure do not adhere to the geopolitical boundaries that define nation-states. Only through coordinated efforts can we hope to address the systemic challenges that arise when technological progress generates exponential increases in resource consumption.

The story of Jevons' Paradox, then, is not merely a cautionary tale from the annals of economic thought, but a living reminder that every stride towards efficiency is paradoxically accompanied by a surge in consumption. From steam engines that consumed more coal as they grew more efficient to modern AI systems that demand ever greater quantities of computational power, the historical pattern remains intact. Yet, within this pattern lies the potential for innovation. If the promise of quantum technology can be realised, it may well transform our economic landscape, ushering in an era where complex problems are solved not through brute computational force but through elegant, energy-efficient quantum algorithms.

However, the road to a quantum future is anything but straightforward. It is fraught with technical and ethical challenges that demand careful consideration. To harness the potential of quantum computing without succumbing to its pitfalls, we must cultivate an approach that is as much about ethical governance as it is about technological innovation. This approach will require the collaborative efforts of scientists, engineers, policymakers, and ethicists - an alliance dedicated to ensuring that progress in the quantum realm does not come at the expense of security, privacy, or environmental sustainability.

Indeed, the emergence of quantum technologies represents one of the most transformative shifts in the history of computing. This shift is not merely incremental but revolutionary, promising to upend the longstanding paradigms that have governed classical computation. Should these quantum breakthroughs manage to scale beyond the confines of experimental labs and into the realm of practical application, they could lead to a dramatic reconfiguration of our digital and economic infrastructures. In such a scenario, the severe limitations imposed by energy-intensive data centres might be mitigated by quantum-enhanced systems that require far less power to perform computationally intensive tasks. Such a transformation would not only address the immediate concerns of energy consumption but could also open new economic vistas by enabling hitherto unimagined applications across science, industry, and everyday life.

Moreover, the economic ramifications of a successful quantum revolution extend well beyond mere operational efficiency. The diffusion of quantum technology could spearhead new industries, create high-skill job opportunities, and redefine competitive advantage on the global stage. Market analysts already suggest that economies which successfully integrate quantum computing into their technological framework may enjoy a substantial head start in areas ranging from pharmaceuticals to cryptography and financial modelling. As governments and corporations pour billions into research and development, the race for quantum supremacy is becoming as intense as any industrial competition witnessed in modern history.

Yet, even as this quantum promise tantalises economists

and technologists alike, it is imperative that we confront its potential pitfalls. The dual-use nature of quantum technology means that while its applications in optimisation and energy efficiency may be beneficial, its capacity to undermine current security protocols also poses severe risks. With the possibility of quantum computers breaking even the most robust encryption algorithms on the horizon, the very notion of cybersecurity stands at a crossroads. In such a dynamic technological landscape, the economic benefits of quantum computing must be carefully weighed against the potential catastrophic societal impacts of compromised data security.

As we examine these intertwined technological, economic, and environmental threads, it becomes evident that the future of artificial intelligence and quantum computing is as much a question of societal values as it is of scientific progress. The promise of virtually limitless computational power is alluring, yet it carries with it the inherent risk of fuelling an unsustainable consumption spiral if not managed with foresight and ethical responsibility. It thereby places upon us a dual mandate: to harness the incredible capacities of these technologies while at the same time instituting robust frameworks - both regulatory and societal - that ensure their deployment benefits humanity as a whole rather than merely accelerating consumption for its own sake.

Reflections on the classical economic theories, such as those proposed by Jevons, remind us that the historical trajectory of innovation is rarely linear. Instead, what we see is a pattern in which each gain in efficiency paradoxically generates new demands, new markets, and ultimately, new challenges. In the digital era, where artificial intelligence is rapidly becoming the new backbone of economic activity, these lessons are particularly salient. Efficiency in technology, much like efficiency in energy consumption during the steam engine era, does not simply lead to a diminution in resource usage; rather, it begets a dynamic ecosystem in which consumption is continually reinvented and amplified.

In considering multiple perspectives – from the intricate workings of semiconductor fabrication to the immense potential of quantum algorithms – we are confronted with the need for a new economic model. One that is flexible, adaptive, and capable of integrating the insights of both classical economic theory and modern technological innovation. Such a model would not only need to account for the immediate benefits of technological efficiency but also for the long-term, systemic impacts on energy consumption, environmental sustainability, and even geopolitics. It is within this context that the debate over the sustainability of artificial intelligence and the promise of quantum computing can be seen not as isolated issues, but as part of a broader conversation about the future of economic growth in an era defined by rapid technological transformation.

The path ahead is undoubtedly complex and fraught with challenges. Yet, history has taught us that human ingenuity often rises to meet even the most daunting of challenges. Just as the industrial pioneers of the nineteenth century and the automotive revolutionaries of the twentieth navigated the tumultuous waters of their respective eras, so too must we now find a way to reconcile the seemingly paradoxical relationship between technological efficiency and consumption. This reconciliation will require not only technical innovation but a deep commitment to ethical stewardship and sustainable economic practices.

As we stand on the cusp of what might be the next great

revolution in computation, it is worth pausing to reflect on the lessons of the past. Jevons' insight - that increased efficiency can lead to greater, not lesser, total consumption - remains a potent reminder of the unintended consequences that often accompany technological progress. In the context of artificial intelligence and quantum computing, this paradox invites us to look beyond the immediate gratification of more powerful processors and faster data centres; it urges us to consider the broader implications for our energy infrastructure, our environmental sustainability, and, ultimately, our collective future.

One might argue that the solution lies in a reimagining of our economic priorities. Rather than pursuing unfettered growth in computational power as an end in itself, perhaps we must begin to see energy efficiency, environmental stewardship, and ethical governance as the true measures of progress in a digital age. It is a future that, while far from guaranteed, beckons with the promise of a more sustainable and equitable world.

In the end, the interplay between technological innovation, economic theory, and environmental sustainability challenges us to rethink what it truly means to progress. It compels us to ask difficult questions: How do we balance the allure of cutting-edge technology with the responsibility we bear to the planet and to future generations? Can our relentless push for efficiency inadvertently lead us down a path of self-destruction through insatiable consumption? And perhaps most importantly, can the revolutionary potential of quantum computing, with its promise of fundamentally altering the principles on which our digital world is built, provide a viable escape route from these dilemmas?

The answers to these questions are neither simple nor immediately apparent. They require a concerted effort from all sectors of society – researchers, policymakers, industry leaders, and citizens alike – to forge a path that respects the lessons of history while embracing the opportunities of the future. Economic models must evolve to incorporate externalities, particularly those related to energy and environmental impact, and technological development must be guided by principles that prioritise both efficiency and sustainability. In doing so, we may yet find a way to harness the immense potential of artificial intelligence and quantum computing without falling prey to the very pitfalls that have dogged technological progress throughout history.

In contemplating the unfolding narrative of our digital age, we are reminded of the inherent tension that lies at the heart of progress. Efficiency and consumption are inexorably linked, and any effort to push the boundaries of what is technologically possible brings with it the spectre of unforeseen consequences. It is within this intricate dance of innovation and adaptation that our future will be written – a future where the promise of quantum computing might, if guided by wisdom and prudence, finally break the vicious cycle that Jevons so astutely observed over a century and a half ago.

As we look ahead, it becomes clear that our journey is not merely one of technological evolution, but of economic and societal transformation as well. The interplay between artificial intelligence, data-centric infrastructures, and quantum computing will shape the contours of our global economy for decades to come. In this context, the challenges posed by energy consumption, environmental sustainability, and ethical governance are not obstacles to be feared, but opportunities to reimagine and reinvent the very foundations of how we live, work, and interact with one another.

The task before us is monumental. We must integrate the insights of economic theory, such as those offered by Jevons, with the breakthroughs of modern science to create systems that are robust, sustainable, and ultimately beneficial for all members of society. It is a challenge that demands innovation not only in technology but in the economic and regulatory frameworks that underpin it. Only by embracing this holistic perspective can we hope to ensure that the advances in artificial intelligence and quantum computing do not merely serve as engines of growth in a narrow sense, but as catalysts for a broader, more sustainable, and ethically sound form of progress.

In drawing these threads together – historical lessons from the Industrial Revolution, the modern realities of data-centred infrastructure, and the emerging promise of quantum computing – we are left with a stark yet hopeful picture. The energy revolution of the nineteenth century, driven by the inexorable logic of Jevons' Paradox, finds its modern counterpart in the digital age. Yet within this narrative lies a glimmer of transformational possibility. The innovations we are witnessing today, from highly efficient processors to the nascent field of quantum computing, may one day enable a new paradigm in which technological growth coexists harmoniously with environmental sustainability and economic resilience.

Indeed, the pathway to such a future is fraught with uncertainty, and the challenges are as varied as they are significant. The economic pressures of a digital world, the environmental toll of ever-increasing energy consumption, and the ethical dilemmas posed by rapid technological change demand that we remain vigilant and adaptive. As the ancient Greek philosopher Aristotle once mused about the nature of flourishing - eudaimonia - we, too, must ensure that our technological endeavours lead not only to greater computational prowess but to a richer, more equitable, and sustainable human experience.

In this era of unprecedented capability, the potential for computing to serve as a turning point in our quest for sustainability is immense. By harnessing the power inherent in quantum mechanics, we may yet find a way to transcend the limitations of classical computation. Such a breakthrough carries with it not only the promise of dramatically reduced energy consumption but also the potential to unlock new realms of economic and scientific discovery. It is a prospect that, if carefully managed, could herald an era of progress that is as responsible as it is revolutionary.

Thus, as we navigate the labyrinthine interplay between efficiency, consumption, and technological innovation, we must keep sight of the broader context. The narrative of our digital era is not solely about pushing the boundaries of what is possible with artificial intelligence or quantum computing; it is about forging a future in which these technologies serve the greater good. It is about ensuring that every leap forward in efficiency is matched by a corresponding commitment to sustainability and ethical stewardship - a commitment that acknowledges the full complexity of our modern economic and environmental challenges.

The journey from 1865 to the present day is a testament to the enduring power of human ingenuity and the constant tension between progress and its unintended consequences. It is, therefore, incumbent upon us not only to celebrate the remarkable achievements of our time but also to engage in thoughtful reflection about the kind of future we wish to build. A future where efficiency does not merely fuel greater consumption, but instead, paves the way for innovation that uplifts humanity while preserving the delicate balance of our natural world. In this light, the evolution of artificial intelligence and the advent of quantum computing are not only technological milestones but milestones in our ongoing journey toward a more enlightened and sustainable civilisation.

In contemplating these vast interconnections - between economic theory, technological innovation, energy consumption, and environmental impact - we are reminded that the challenges of the twenty-first century require nothing less than a fundamental rethinking of how we approach progress. The very tools that have enabled us to reach the stars and explore the deepest recesses of digital space now call upon us to also safeguard the foundations of life on Earth. As we stand at this crossroads, the choices we make in shaping our digital and economic futures will echo for generations to come, defining not only the nature of our technologies but the trajectory of our shared destiny.

Ultimately, whether through the incremental improvements in conventional computing or the transformative promise of quantum systems, the imperative is clear: we must devise solutions that are capable of transcending the paradox of efficiency, harnessing innovation for the greater collective good while ensuring that our energy appetite is met in a manner that does not compromise the sustainability of our world. Only thus can we hope to emerge from the cycle of consumption unscathed, and instead, foster an era of responsible, sustainable progress that honours the lessons of history while bravely charting a course into the future.

In a world where every technological leap is accompanied by complex challenges, the fusion of economic insight, scientific endeavour, and ethical governance offers our best hope for overcoming the paradoxes that have long defined the relationship between efficiency and consumption. As we continue to deploy artificial intelligence, expand our digital infrastructures, and explore the immense potential of quantum computing, we must do so with an unwavering commitment to creating a balanced and sustainable future - one that benefits not just the few, but all of humanity.

III

Integrity and the Corporate Culture

8

The Value of Integrity in Leadership

Integrity is the steady and unyielding foundation upon which true leadership is built. It is that core quality that transforms mere authority into a force for genuine progress and lasting impact. Without integrity, vision is reduced to manipulation, strategy morphs into deception, and the very influence a leader wields risks turning into nothing more than coercion and exploitation. History is replete with examples of those who wielded power without the guiding light of integrity, and time and again, such leadership has ultimately proved to be nothing more than a delicate illusion destined to crumble under the weight of scrutiny. To lead with integrity is not simply to recite the truth or to maintain a squeaky-clean record; it is to embody truth through every action undertaken and every decision made, standing resolutely by one's principles regardless of the temptations of expediency that often offer more immediate and seemingly easier routes.

Throughout the ages, great thinkers have debated what it means to live a virtuous life - a life marked by consistency, honour, and moral clarity. Aristotle, whose thoughts on ethics continue to resonate through the centuries, argued that integrity is not a one-off choice or an occasional act of righteousness but rather a cultivated habit. In his view, virtues are habits that must be continuously honed through deliberate action and practice - integrity being among the most important of these virtues. Aristotle saw a clear distinction between cleverness, known as one's ability to manoeuvre through complexity and seize opportunity, and true wisdom, which is inherently moral in nature. While cleverness can serve as a useful tool, it is neutral in moral calibre and, when detached from ethical guidance, can descend into cunning manipulation that leaves a legacy as unstable as it is morally questionable. True wisdom, conversely, is not simply a demonstration of intellectual power; it is a deep and abiding commitment to the good. It ensures that every action, every strategic move, is harmonised with ethical principles, allowing even the most innovative ideas and dominant visions to be implemented in ways that are both effective and deeply just.

Indeed, integrity emerges as much more than a professional requirement in the realm of leadership; it is a fundamental condition for real human excellence, shaping both private lives and public endeavours alike. It is the north star that guides leaders through tumultuous times toward decisions that contribute to genuine and enduring prosperity, not just for themselves, but for the communities that lean on their guidance. Embracing integrity means choosing a path where values and actions walk hand in hand. It means resisting the allure of shortcuts that may appear beneficial in the short term but are fraught with ethical compromise. This steadfast approach to truth and moral clarity is what distinguishes leaders who inspire lasting trust from those whose influence is ephemeral, built on shifting sands of opportunism and self-interest.

When one delves deeper into the philosophical underpinnings of integrity, the contributions of great thinkers such as Plato, Aristotle, Kant, and Socrates become particularly illuminating.

Plato's writings, for instance, provide a rich tapestry that interweaves the pursuit of intellectual and moral virtue. Although Plato does not always use the modern term "integrity," the concept permeates his discussions on the harmony of the soul and the structure of an ideal society. In Plato's dialogues, especially in works like The Republic, the nature of justice is explored through the lens of virtue and the orchestration of different parts of the soul. Plato posited that the soul is comprised of three distinct parts: the rational, the spirited, and the appetitive. The rational part is that which seeks wisdom, perspective, and an understanding of eternal truths. The spirited or courageous part is what fuels one's sense of honour and initiative, prompting actions in defence of what is just and right. And then there is the appetitive part, representative of the body's desires for pleasure and material fulfilment. When these elements align harmoniously under the guidance of reason, a person achieves a state of integrity where every action resonates with the internal order of their character. Plato's allegory of the charioteer governing two horses, one noble and obedient, the other wild and uncontrollable, paints a vivid picture of what it means to maintain such equilibrium. For Plato, the leader - the philosopher-king - was to be a person who had achieved mastery over these inner conflicts, permitting reason to guide passion rather than let impulsivity and base desires override inner wisdom. Integrity, in this classical sense, was synonymous with internal order, moral clarity, and the alignment of one's inner nature with the universal principles of truth and justice.

Aristotle, following a similar yet distinct path, advanced the idea that virtues, including integrity, are not acquired through isolated acts, but through the repetition of morally sound choices. In his ethical framework, he discussed the importance of developing habits that solidify as character traits over time. Just as a craftsman refines his art through continual practice, so too must a leader cultivate habits of integrity by repeatedly aligning actions with deeply held ethical convictions. Aristotle emphasised that even in the face of temptations, where the easier course might lead to immediate gains but compromise one's moral compass, it is the commitment to virtuous action that sets a leader apart. An individual who demonstrates integrity is not only abiding by rules for their own sake but is also constantly refining a character that is robust enough to withstand external pressures and internal conflicts alike.

Similarly, the moral philosophy of Immanuel Kant underscores the central role of integrity in ethical decision-making. Kant's categorical imperative commands that one should act only according to the maxim that they wish to see become a universal law. This principle forces leaders to consider whether their actions, if universally applied, would contribute to a just and moral society. For a leader, this means that every choice must be scrutinised not only for its immediate consequences, but also for the broader impact it would have if adopted by all. Integrity, then, becomes a test of moral clarity and self-discipline - a refusal to compromise ethical norms even when it might be expedient or beneficial in the short term. Under

Kant's framework, the true measure of a leader is not found in the efficacy of their decisions alone but in the unwavering commitment to principles that elevate the common good above personal or institutional gain.

Socrates, the revered father of Western philosophy, also offers timeless insights into the value of integrity. Known for his relentless pursuit of truth and his method of questioning assumptions, Socrates believed that *an unexamined life was not worth living.* His insistence on constant self-scrutiny highlights integrity as a continuous process of aligning one's beliefs and actions with the pursuit of truth. Socrates challenged those in power to engage in deep, introspective dialogue about the nature of justice and the responsibilities of leadership. Even when faced with the risk of persecution, his commitment to truth never wavered – an exemplar of integrity that stands in stark contrast to leaders who shy away from moral accountability when the stakes are high. The Socratic method teaches that integrity is not a static quality but rather an active and dynamic engagement with one's inner moral compass, a quality that is essential for anyone who bears the mantle of leadership.

When these philosophical perspectives are woven into the fabric of leadership, the connection is unmistakable: integrity lies at the heart of effective and ethical leadership. It is the very quality that transforms a position of power into an opportunity for positive influence and enduring impact. Integrity ensures that leaders remain true to their principles, honour the trust placed in them by their followers, and make decisions that uphold the greater good, even when the easier path might lead to personal benefit or short-term success. Without such integrity, leaders risk undermining not only their own moral standing but also the collective trust and cohesion of the communities, organisations, and nations they are called to serve.

This commitment to integrity is perhaps most vividly illustrated in times of crisis. Systems built on shaky ethical ground can appear stable in periods of peace and prosperity, yet it is during moments of adversity that the true measure of leadership is revealed. Reflecting on historical episodes, one need only consider the marvellous example set by Ernest Shackleton - a leader who found himself and his men stranded amidst the icy wilderness of the Antarctic. In such dire circumstances, the path of least resistance might have been to prioritise personal survival over collective welfare. Yet Shackleton's deep-seated integrity compelled him to choose a more arduous road: one where every decision was weighed against the standard of unwavering commitment to his men. His leadership was not marked by grandiose declarations, but by the quiet and steadfast alignment of his actions with his promises. His crew, recognising this consistency and moral fortitude, followed him out of respect and trust rather than mere hierarchical obligation. Such stories remind us that true leadership is not measured solely by the ability to achieve tactical victories but by the strength of character that inspires collective trust and mutual respect across all levels of an organisation or society.

In the modern era, the imperative to lead with integrity is coming into sharp focus, especially within fields that are evolving as rapidly as the energy sector. The global shift towards sustainable energy is not merely a technical transition; it represents a profound challenge for leadership. The energy industry is a realm of competing priorities - balancing the demands of environmental stewardship and economic viability, short-term profitability and long-term sustainability. Leaders in this sphere confront complex and often conflicting stakeholder interests. Without an unshakeable commitment to integrity, even the most well-intentioned efforts may devolve into platforms for deceptive practices, such as greenwashing, where superficial commitments to sustainability mask a deeper prioritisation of profit over principle. For energy leaders, as for all leaders, the core challenge remains consistent: fostering genuine, ethically driven progress that recognises the intrinsic value of truth and transparency in every decision made, regardless of the potential short-term rewards sacrificed.

Reflecting on the insights of contemporary leadership experts, one finds that figures such as Bill George, former CEO of Medtronic, have echoed the timeless truth that authentic leadership is driven by an internal compass of purpose and integrity. Authentic leaders are not motivated by external accolades or fleeting recognition; rather, they are guided by an unwavering sense of purpose that aligns every decision with the broader commitment to the common good. When leaders abandon this internal compass - when they allow political expediency, self-interest, or fleeting commercial interests to override their commitment to truth - they ultimately compromise not only their own reputations but also the foundations upon which their organisations are built. The case of corporate scandals and political debacles across the globe serves as a stark reminder of how quickly the absence of integrity can erode trust and lead to catastrophic outcomes.

Equally important is the role that empathy plays in reinforcing the connection between integrity and leadership. A leader who demonstrates genuine integrity must also be attuned to the human implications of their choices. Empathy, the capacity to understand and share the feelings of others, does not detract from a commitment to robust ethical standards; rather, it complements it. Without empathy, integrity risks devolving into an inflexible adherence to rules, potentially disregarding the situational nuances that characterise real-world dilemmas. Consider the example of Ernest Shackleton once more: his decisions were grounded not only in an objective adherence to principle but also in a profound understanding of the needs and vulnerabilities of his crew. Similarly, contemporary leaders like Warren Buffett and Jacinda Ardern have shown that empathy - when integrated with a steadfast commitment to transparency and accountability - serves as a powerful stabilising force in both business and politics. By integrating empathy with integrity, great leaders are able to navigate complex moral landscapes in a manner that is both just and deeply humane.

Another dimension of integrity that demands recognition is its inherent resilience. Leaders who compromise their principles for short-term gains may experience brief successes, but history teaches us that such achievements are invariably brittle, destined to crumble under the strain of inevitable contradictions and external challenges. The ruin of Napoleon's empire serves as a stark illustration of this truth. Although widely recognised as a military genius, Napoleon's eventual downfall was precipitated not by a lack of strategic acumen but by a fundamental breach of trust with his men and his nation. His leadership transformed from a force of transformative innovation into a personal myth, one that increasingly obscured the harsh realities of his regime. His inability - or unwillingness - to remain anchored to ethical principles ultimately undermined the social and moral fabric that had once supported his ambitions. This cautionary tale resonates in today's world, reminding us that leaders who allow integrity to be compromised, however slightly, risk not only their own legacy but also the broader stability and trust upon which their followers depend.

In grappling with the expansive challenge of maintaining integrity in leadership, one must consider that the path is neither linear nor free from conflict. The greatest challenge of the 21st century is not solely in technological advances or economic competition, but in the preservation and reinvigoration of ethical leadership. As transformative forces such as artificial intelligence reshape industries and the global energy paradigm undergoes a profound metamorphosis, the need for leaders who conduct themselves with unwavering integrity becomes ever more critical. In these rapidly changing environments, clear-eyed ethical vision is required to steer through uncharted terrains without abandoning the principles that ensure fairness, justice, and sustainability.

It is through this lens of ethical resilience that the teachings of philosophers like Aristotle, Kant, Plato, and Socrates continue to offer invaluable insights. Their ideas are not relics of a bygone era; rather, they are living principles that provide guidance and a moral framework within which modern leaders can find direction. Aristotle's assertion that excellence is not a singular act but a habit underscores the need for consistency in moral choices. Kant's categorical imperative invites leaders to conduct a continuous internal evaluation - asking whether every action taken could be deemed acceptable if it were universalised as a guiding principle for all. Such reflective practices are essential for leaders who aim to leave behind not only a legacy of success but also a legacy of transcendence in ethical standards.

Plato's vision, with its profound illustration of the inner workings of the soul and the allegory of the charioteer, challenges us to continually strive for internal harmony - a state where reason, courage, and desire are not in a constant struggle but are harmoniously integrated. Such balance is especially imperative in leadership, where the pressure to deliver results can often lead to shortcuts and compromises. Only those who have cultivated the internal discipline to maintain such balance can hope to make decisions that are both visionary and ethically unequivocal.

Socrates' method of relentless self-questioning and his insistence on the examined life prompt every leader to foster a culture of continuous moral reflection. It is through such introspection that the seeds of integrity are nurtured, ensuring that every leadership decision is the product of careful deliberation rather than impulsive reaction. In an era where rapid decision-making is often prized, the time-honoured wisdom of Socrates serves as a reminder that integrity is forged in moments of reflection and that true leadership demands an ongoing commitment to understanding and truth.

Taking these philosophical lessons into account, it becomes clear that integrity is far more than a personal or professional attribute - it is the organisational bedrock upon which the sustainable success of any endeavour rests. The energy transition, for instance, exemplifies the need for absolute ethical clarity. As industries navigate a future where sustainable practices must replace old models of profit-driven exploitation, the presence of leaders with unshakeable integrity is paramount. Energy leaders who prioritise long-term societal benefits, transparency, and environmental stewardship over short-term gains are the ones who will not only drive technological innovations but also secure the social licence to operate in an increasingly conscientious global market.

This principle is equally applicable across all domains of leadership, whether one is steering multinational corporations, managing political institutions, or guiding non-profit organisations. Integrity, when it is allowed to take root at the heart of an organisation, transforms business practices and societal dynamics. It creates a culture where every decision, every strategy, and every interaction is guided by a resolute commitment to the public good. Its effects are multiplicative, fostering trust among stakeholders, enhancing the credibility of institutions, and ultimately contributing to the collective good. Conversely, the erosion of integrity - whether through overt dishonesty, subtle manipulation, or moral compromise - can have cascading negative effects that undermine the very foundations of leadership and community.

In the realm of contemporary leadership, we see countless examples where the commitment to integrity has yielded transformative change. Political leaders like Jacinda Ardern have demonstrated that even in the turbulent arena of international politics, where pressures are immense and the stakes are high, a leader committed to empathy, transparency, and principled action can engender widespread trust and solidarity. Similarly, in the business realm, figures such as Warren Buffett have long been lauded not merely for their financial acumen but for their steadfast adherence to ethical practices and the cultivation of an organisational culture that places integrity at its core. These examples reinforce an enduring truth: that integrity, when embedded in the fabric of leadership, engenders a ripple effect of trust, commitment, and long-term stability that benefits all involved.

Moreover, the modern digital age poses new challenges and opportunities for leaders striving to maintain integrity. The rapid spread of information through social media, the phenomenon of 'fake news', and the increasing demand for transparency from a sceptical public all underscore the necessity for leaders who not only speak the truth but also live it consistently. In this context, integrity becomes a bulwark against the temptations of sensationalism and the lure of expedient yet misleading tactics. Leaders who repeatedly demonstrate a commitment to transparency and factual correctness establish a moral credibility that serves as both an anchor and a beacon in times of uncertainty. This trust, once established, can be the decisive factor in rallying support, fostering loyalty, and inspiring collective action towards shared goals.

The journey to cultivating integrity is, however, fraught with challenges. It demands constant vigilance and a willingness to subject oneself to rigorous self-examination. Every decision, no matter how trivial it may seem at the time, becomes a test of character. In an interconnected world where actions are scrutinised on a global scale, the smallest deviation from ethical conduct can be magnified, potentially undermining years of hard-won trust. Yet it is precisely in this challenging environment that the true essence of integrity is revealed. Leaders who are unwavering in their commitment to moral principles, even under the most adverse circumstances, demonstrate a fortitude that surpasses mere rhetoric. Their actions affirm that integrity is not a liability in the face of hardship but the very quality that enables one to navigate crises with judicious care and steadfast resolve.

As we examine the plethora of challenges that modern

leaders face – be it in the realm of the energy transition, global commerce, or international diplomacy – the call for integrity becomes ever more urgent. The accelerating pace of technological change, coupled with the persistent inequalities and ethical dilemmas that mark our age, mandates that leadership be rooted in a balanced and principled approach. Leaders must rise above the prevailing currents of opportunism and short-termism, embracing instead a long-term vision that honours the principles of justice, equity, and sustainability. This is not an easy path; it requires sacrifice, self-discipline, and a willingness to put the collective good above individual or corporate gain. And yet, history has shown again and again that the leaders who choose this path – who combine intellectual rigour with moral clarity – are the ones who leave an indelible mark on society.

It is instructive to reflect on the broader implications of integrity in the context of leadership beyond mere organisational success. Integrity has a profound social resonance. It builds bridges of trust within communities, fosters cooperation across adversarial divides, and creates a fertile ground for collective progress. When leaders act with unwavering integrity, they send a message that transcends the immediate circumstances – a message that truth and ethical conduct can prevail even in the face of adversity. This, in turn, inspires others to adopt similar standards, setting in motion a positive cycle where societal norms gradually shift towards greater transparency and accountability. In this way, integrity is not a solitary virtue confined to the decisions of a few; it is a societal imperative that shapes the very character of communities and nations alike.

In contemplating the enduring importance of integrity, one

must also consider the risk of moral relativity that modern leadership can sometimes encounter. In an era where the boundaries of acceptable behaviour are often blurred by the exigencies of the moment, the temptation to justify questionable tactics in the name of expediency can be overwhelming. Yet it is precisely in these moments that the principles articulated by Aristotle, Kant, Plato, and Socrates offer a counterpoint to the erosion of moral standards. Integrity, viewed through their timeless insights, is not a negotiable commodity but a non-derogable pillar of human excellence. A leader who compromises even a fraction of this commitment ultimately risks more than just their own reputation – it endangers the very fabric of the institution they lead and the broader trust that holds society together.

History reminds us time and again that while leaders who sacrifice integrity might enjoy fleeting triumphs, the long-term consequences are invariably dire. The narratives of fallen empires, ruined reputations, and societies engulfed in corruption serve as stern warnings. Conversely, the legacy of leaders who have maintained an unassailable commitment to truth, fairness, and ethical conduct is immortalised in the annals of history – not merely for their successes in achieving material ends, but for their ability to inspire a higher standard of conduct in those who followed. These leaders become symbols of moral courage and exemplars of what it truly means to lead. Their legacy, built on the bedrock of integrity, continues to shape societies long after their time, providing a beacon for future generations grappling with the complexities of leadership in an increasingly volatile world.

The theme of integrity is both timeless and indispensable. The ancient philosophies converge on the notion that integrity is essential for not only personal excellence but also for effective and enduring leadership. From Plato's allegory of the charioteer steering a soul in harmonious balance to Aristotle's insistence on the cultivation of virtue through habitual, conscientious action, from Kant's categorical imperative demanding that every action be worthy of universalisation to Socrates' relentless quest for truth and self-knowledge, the message is unmistakable: integrity is the ultimate currency of leadership. It is what transforms a leader from a mere holder of power into a custodian of hope, a guardian of justice, and a catalyst for societal progress.

As we witness unprecedented global challenges - from the transformation of energy systems to the rapid evolution of technology and the pressing need for sustainable development - the call for leaders who are unwavering in their commitment to integrity becomes ever clearer. It is a call to return to the fundamentals of ethical leadership, to reject the allure of facile shortcuts and expedient deceptions, and instead to embrace a path of truth, accountability, and constant self-improvement. Only by doing so can we hope to develop a future where progress is not measured solely by tangible achievements but by the quality of the leadership that guides us towards a more just and equitable world.

Ultimately, integrity is the very essence of what it means to be a leader of character. It is the quiet strength that underpins bold decisions, the moral compass that guides institutions through turbulent times, and the inexhaustible source of trust upon which communities are built. In the modern world, where the pressures of expediency and the temptations of self-interest are ever-present, the need for integrity in leadership is more urgent than ever. As we continue to navigate the complexities of the 21st century, let us remember that true leadership does not lie in the mere exercise of authority, but in the consistent, principled pursuit of the common good.

In the end, the legacy of any leader is not solely measured by the magnitude of their achievements, but by the enduring trust they inspire and the moral example they set. Leaders who embrace integrity transform not only their own lives but also the lives of those they lead, creating a ripple effect of positive change that transcends time and circumstance. Their commitment to truth, honour, and ethical action stands as a testament to the power of integrity – a quality that remains as essential today as it was in the times of Plato, and will continue to be the guiding light for all who seek to lead with purpose and passion.

9

The Curious Case of Corporate Culture
– A Satire

Once upon a time, in the sprawling maze of polished corridors and glass-walled conference rooms of GlobalTechyy Enterprises, there emerged a peculiar realm that was as unpredictable as it was omnipresent. It was a world of whispered affirmations and unspoken codes – a world governed not by the CEO's direct orders or the lofty declarations on mission statement posters, but by an unseen, ineffable force: the corporate culture.

It was a bright Monday morning when Maria, a junior anthropologist freshly recruited by GlobalTechy, stepped into this vibrant microcosm. With her keen eye for human rituals and a mischievous curiosity that reminded her of the early explorers of ancient tribes, Maria was determined to uncover the mystique of what many in the company coyly referred to as "the vibe." She quickly discovered that corporate culture was not merely a set of abstract ideals plastered on the boardroom walls – it was a living, breathing entity, much like the tribal customs studied by her academic mentors in dusty university archives.

Maria's first encounter with this invisible force happened in the grand atrium - a space that resembled an ancient assembly hall, complete with strategically placed inspirational posters that glowed like modern-day hieroglyphs. Here, a diverse congregation of bright-eyed optimists, battle-hardened veterans of the corporate jungle, and a motley array of individuals who had mastered the art of feigning busyness congregated each morning. They were a modern tribe, each person embodying a distinct role in a grand narrative that was part spiritual journey, part survival of the fittest.

At the helm of this bustling society stood Richard, the enigmatic CEO whose presence loomed large over the company like a shamanic figure. Richard was a man of contradictions - a visionary preaching disruption, synergy, and the miraculous promise of artificial intelligence, yet often found himself adrift in a sea of buzzwords that had little substance beyond their sound. At the weekly leadership summit held in a cavernous meeting room adorned with sleek tech and minimalist art, Richard would stand before his assembly and declare, with the fervor of a tribal elder, "Our culture is what sets us apart! It's what defines us!" His voice would echo against the walls, resonating with an authority that left little room for dissent, even as the employees exchanged knowing glances that betrayed their inner skepticism.

The weekly meetings, Maria soon learned, were more than just a forum for passing orders - they were elaborate performances of language and ritual. In these gatherings, words such as 'alignment,' 'scalability,' and 'paradigm shift' were tossed around with an almost mystical reverence, as if each syllable contained the secret to mystical industrial success. Middle managers, decked out in meticulously prepared PowerPoint presentations that could lull the most alert mind into a trance, became the modern equivalent of wandering bards reciting verses of a forgotten epic. The employees, in a display of ritualistic nodding and carefully measured expressions, participated in this spectacle, their silent compliance serving to reinforce the collective myth of the company.

It was during one of these sessions that Maria began to perceive the true nature of this corporate culture. Like the early anthropologists who had documented the rites and customs of remote tribes, she started mapping out the subtle nuances of the behaviour around her. She observed a curious juxtaposition: despite the seemingly coherent language of synergy and innovation, there existed an undercurrent of absurdity that pervaded even the most serious of discussions. When a new initiative was introduced - often indistinguishable from its predecessors - the crowd would almost unanimously agree, as if a hidden signal had compelled them. No one dared to question the rationale behind the proposals, for in the realm of corporate culture, questioning was akin to disrupting a sacred ritual.

Yet, as Maria delved deeper into the labyrinth of GlobalTechy, a new phenomenon began to ripple through the tribe - one that blended modernity with ancient echoes of technology. It started innocuously enough: the integration of artificial intelligence into the fabric of daily operations. Initially, AI was introduced as a mere assistant, handling mundane tasks like generating automated reports and crunching data with machine-like efficiency. Like a silent scribe in an ancient court, the AI processed information, never tiring, never complaining, and never deviating from its programmed purpose.

Before long, however, the AI began to infiltrate more personal and sensitive realms of the corporate existence. Performance evaluations, once the domain of thoughtful human judgment, were now being augmented by algorithms that calculated "engagement levels" - a new metric measured by the frequency of after-hours email responses and the speed with which one clicked 'reply.' The HR department, ever anxious in its bid to sustain the delicate equilibrium of the company's culture, introduced "AI Empathy Sessions." These sessions were designed as communal gatherings where employees were urged to reflect upon and share their feelings about the creeping ubiquity of technology. Much like the tribal councils where elders solicited opinions on matters of communal lore, these meetings, however, were fraught with an eerie silence as few dared to voice their genuine concerns, and even fewer expected that their words might alter the course of an ever-evolving narrative.

One incident, in particular, caught Maria's scholarly attention. It was the annual corporate retreat - a storied event designed to "reignite passion and collaboration" within the tribe. The retreat was a paradox, a modern ritual that, instead of bonding the group, often left its participants mired in awkward conversations and existential self-doubt. The previous year's retreat had been provocatively themed "The Future is Now." In an audacious attempt to merge the wisdom of old with the allure of futuristic promise, senior executives had shared the stage with a humanoid AI assistant known as ALFIE. During a panel discussion intended to forecast the company's destiny, ALFIE, with its gleaming metallic visage and unnaturally calm tone, had delivered responses that outshone even the most polished human remarks. The panel, visibly unnerved by the AI's superior articulation, found themselves at a rare loss for words - a moment that resonated with irony, as the attendees departed from the retreat not with newfound inspiration but with a lingering sense of disquiet about the very essence of leadership and knowledge.

Despite the occasional flashes of absurdity and the creeping infiltration of AI, GlobalTechy pressed on with a fervor that bordered on ritualistic devotion. The upper echelons of leadership, in their infinite wisdom, decreed that the cure for any malaise was a renewed commitment to what they termed "culture-first" strategies. More town halls were arranged, their frequency rivaling that of the tribal gatherings of old. Breakrooms were soon festooned with inspirational quotes and vivid murals aimed at invoking feelings of unity and shared purpose. In a move that would have delighted Kafka himself, the Human Resources department rolled out a mandatory "Culture Fit Assessment." The survey was a labyrinth of questions where the only acceptable answer was an unwavering "strongly agree," reinforcing an eerie homogeneity that left little room for dissent or genuine reflection.

At the center of this grand ritual, Richard remained an enigmatic figure. His declarations, filled with grandiloquence and fervent idealism, were repeated like liturgical mantras during his oratory in all-hands meetings. "Our culture is our greatest asset!" he would proclaim, his eyes gleaming with the conviction of someone who believed that the spirit of the tribe was his to command. But beneath the veneer of corporate pride lay a paradox: the very culture Richard championed had, over time, become entangled in an intricate web of mimicry and repetition. It was as if every policy, every buzzword, had been absorbed by an ever-thriving machine that ensured the preservation of a status quo – a machine that, unknowingly to Richard, was powered by none other than artificial intelligence.

Amidst all these grand orchestrations, one individual emerged as both an accidental rebel and an unlikely hero in the unfolding drama. Charlie, a lowly intern with an irreverent streak and an insatiable curiosity about the inner workings of the corporate beast, decided one day to test the boundaries of the established order. With a mischievous glint in his eye that betrayed his deep understanding of the system's absurdities, Charlie began to code an AI chatbot in the quiet solitude of his cramped cubicle. This was no ordinary piece of software – it was an ingenious device that could generate leadership jargon in real time, saturating the company's internal systems with a flood of buzzwords and seemingly profound statements.

When Charlie boldly presented his creation as "an innovative tool for enhancing executive communication" during one of the notoriously dreary Monday morning meetings, the reaction was instantaneous. Richard, ever on the lookout for cutting-edge initiatives, was thoroughly enchanted by the chatbot's output. Its phrases flowed effortlessly, and the leadership team, caught up in the performance, was too enamored to notice that the machine's language was virtually indistinguishable from their own carefully choreographed rhetoric. In a masterstroke of irony, the chatbot was quickly integrated into the corporate communication channels. Reports, strategic plans, and even internal memos began to be authored almost entirely by the cold, precise algorithms of this digital wordsmith. And the remarkable thing was that no one noticed the change – after all, the language was the same, the messaging was the same, and the culture had, in its strange way, been perfectly preserved by the very machine that sought to transform it.

As the weeks turned into months, GlobalTechy continued to march forward on what now seemed like a predetermined path of cultural evolution. The employees, with their ritualistic nods and carefully calibrated responses, carried on in a manner that was both mundane and profound. They attended endless meetings where the air was thick with the weight of shared beliefs and carefully rehearsed platitudes. They participated in digitally orchestrated debates about innovation and accountability, unaware that the true master of ceremonies was not a person at all, but an algorithm quietly reshaping the narrative of their daily lives.

Maria, whose journey through this corporate world had grown from academic curiosity to passionate involvement, began to document her observations in a long and increasingly detailed manuscript. She drew fascinating parallels between the corporate rituals she witnessed and the customs of early human societies. Just as ancient tribes developed elaborate myths and legends to explain the mysteries of nature, so too had corporations woven their own intricate stories to justify every decision, every policy, and every strategic pivot. In her writings, Maria likened the mandatory "Culture Fit Assessments" to initiation rites performed by tribal elders - a test designed not merely to measure competence, but to signal to the group that one belonged to the sacred lineage of insiders who understood the unspoken rules.

She noted that, much like the ancient practice of oral storytelling, the true essence of corporate culture was transmitted not through formal documentation, but through everyday interactions. It was in the hushed conversations over lukewarm coffee in the breakroom, the conspiratorial smiles exchanged during PowerPoint presentations, and the ironic chuckles shared amongst colleagues when buzzwords were thrown around as if they were sacrosanct relics of modern wisdom. In global terms, the phenomenon was a striking reminder of what cognitive anthropologists had long observed: that culture, both ancient and modern, emerged organically from thousands of micro-interactions rather than decrees handed down from above.

The paradox of corporate culture, as Maria so eloquently recorded in her journal, was that while companies like Global-Techy invested vast resources in sculpting an idealised version of themselves - a glossy, aspirational image intended to inspire loyalty and dedication - the true power of culture lay in its organic evolution. The official narratives, with their catch-phrases and mandated positivity, were often at odds with what happened behind closed doors. In the quiet corners of the office, employees innovated their own survival strategies, adopting workarounds and unofficial networks that often contradicted the corporate line. The tension between the "official culture" and the "actual culture" created a dynamic, ever-adaptive system, one that was both resilient and, at times, humorously contradictory.

One particularly memorable episode underscored this tension. During yet another quarterly town hall, Richard introduced a sweeping new initiative intended to promote "transparency and openness." Animated graphs, colorful charts, and inspiring videos filled the presentation. Yet, as the meeting drew to a close, an undercurrent of bemusement could be detected among the attendees. After all, transparency in this context meant a series of meticulously rehearsed soundbites and scripted endorsements, rather than a genuine invitation to discuss the real challenges faced by the employees. It was akin to a tribal ritual where the elders recited the sacred texts, even as the common folk whispered alternative interpretations in the safety of the shadows.

It was at this juncture that Maria's reflections took on an even more nuanced tone. Her anthropological lens allowed her to see parallels between the corporate world and the ancient tribes she had read about in dusty field reports. In those early societies, rituals and myths were not mere distractions but essential mechanisms for maintaining cohesion and reinforcing group identity. Today, GlobalTechy's management - perhaps unwittingly - employed similar techniques. The proliferation of inspirational posters, the rigorously choreographed meetings, and even the practice of awarding promotions based on esoteric indicators of "engagement" were all part of a broader strategy to weave a tapestry of shared beliefs and behaviors. Just as ancient societies used symbolic actions to connect their members to a larger cosmic order, so too did the corporate elite at GlobalTechy mobilize cultural symbols to tie their employees to the company's ever-shifting narrative.

Charlie, the intern whose prankish AI chatbot had unintentionally become a linchpin in the corporate narrative, came to embody this fusion of humor and subversion. His quiet rebellion had not only exposed the inherent absurdity of a system obsessed with buzzwords but also revealed a deeper truth: that the culture of the company, for all its grand proclamations, was but a series of predictable, repetitive behaviors. In one unforgettable boardroom meeting, as executives marveled at the refined output of the chatbot, Charlie sat quietly in the back, a knowing smile tugging at his lips. His promotion, which came not as a reward for his technical wizardry but as a side effect of the AI's algorithm marking him as "highly engaged," was a silent testament to the fact that, in a system where even the culture could be coded, the rules of the game were themselves fluid and, at times, comically arbitrary.

As weeks turned into months, an air of both resignation and quiet amusement settled over GlobalTechy. The corridors that once rang with rousing declarations of innovation now echoed with a subtler melody - a mixture of deliberate mimicry and spontaneous humor. Employees had learned that the corporate culture, for all its ostensible profundity, was built on conventions that could be bent, twisted, or even outright mocked without incurring the strict censure reserved for actual breaches of protocol. In hushed conversations over communal lunches, colleagues recounted bizarre anecdotes of former managers who had taken the "culture" mandate to absurd extremes; one story involved an overzealous team leader mandating that every meeting be opened with an interpretative dance - an event that, while initially ridiculed, had since become a cherished, if unofficial, tradition among a select group of daring individuals.

Maria's manuscript, steadily growing with every observation, began to capture the spirit of this evolving cultural landscape. She wove in insights drawn from the studies of renowned anthropologists who had dedicated their lives to understanding early human societies. They had observed that rituals, myths, and infantile narratives were not vestigial relics but indispensable tools for social cohesion. In much the same way, the corporate rituals at GlobalTechy - no matter how contrived they might seem - served to provide a semblance of order and meaning in an otherwise chaotic environment. The clever interplay between human spontaneity and machine efficiency became a living laboratory for exploring the dynamics of modern culture. It was as if the company existed at the crossroads of old-world mysticism and the relentless march of technological progress.

One brisk autumn day, GlobalTechy organised another town hall meeting. This time, the atmosphere was charged with an odd mix of anticipation and resigned humour. Executives clung to their well-rehearsed scripts as they laid out yet another round of initiatives aimed at "reinventing our collective mindset." However, the audience had by now learned to look beyond the polished verbiage. They exchanged subtle winks and shared knowing smiles - an unspoken acknowledgment that, despite the grand pronouncements, the day-to-day reality remained stubbornly unchanged. In this setting, every buzzword and every carefully curated statistic took on a dual existence: one as an official decree and one as a subject of private, often humorous, commentary.

As the meeting wound down and employees filtered out into the corridors, Maria stayed behind a while longer. She lingered near a large window that overlooked the city skyline, reflecting on the fascinating tapestry of human rituals unfolding before her eyes. In that moment, she recalled her academic training in the annals of early anthropology - a field that had taught her that the most enduring cultures were those that evolved organically, shaped by countless small acts of defiance, joke-laden subversions, and genuine human interactions. GlobalTechy, with all its pomp and circumstance, was in essence no different from an ancient society coming to terms with the inevitability of change. It was a vibrant amalgamation of hope, irony, and persistence – a living example of how cultural evolution was an endless process of adaptation, rebellion, and sometimes, unexpected humor.

In the ensuing months, Maria's writings gained attention not only within GlobalTechy's corridors but also among external scholars and industry insiders curious about the intersection of corporate life and anthropological theory. Her detailed accounts of spontaneous rituals, quirky employee behaviours, and subtle forms of resistance turned into a minor sensation, earning her invitations to speak at conferences and panel discussions. One such event, held in a quaint lecture hall adorned with relics from past civilisations, saw Maria drawing parallels between the secret languages of office politics and the oral traditions of ancient tribes. She explained that just as early societies developed myths to explain natural phenomena, modern organizations constructed their own narratives – narratives that were both ingenious and occasionally laughable in their predictability.

The discussion soon turned to the role of technology in this ongoing saga of cultural adaptation. Maria cited the rise of AI as a particularly compelling chapter in the company's story. The integration of artificial intelligence into every facet of work life, from routine reporting to high-level decision-making, was a transformative force that both fascinated and unsettled the tribe. She described how the chatbot, originally a playful gimmick by an intern named Charlie, had been institutionalised so seamlessly that many executives now relied on its generated content without a second thought. In a humorous aside, she noted that it wasn't uncommon for employees to joke that the company's most profound statements were now "decreed by a robot, blessed by our ancestors' unspoken codes." This blend of reverence for technology and a sly nod to the absurd had become the new mantra for the office - a reminder that, in the grand dance of progress, sometimes the most cutting-edge innovations could inadvertently mirror the old ways.

The paradox, as Maria eloquently concluded in her presentation, was that while GlobalTechy's leadership fervently propagated a culture of innovation and boundless possibility, the everyday reality was steeped in an unmistakable sense of continuity - a cultural continuity that defied dramatic reinvention. The employees had internalized a set of shared behaviours and unwritten rules that persisted even as external appearances shifted. It was, in many ways, a testament to the resilient nature of human social structures, echoing the lessons learned from ancient societies where rituals were passed down through generations, often with the same fervour and the same doses of gentle humour.

One memorable episode from that period involved a rather comical misadventure during what was touted as a "Culture Immersion Day," designed to allow new hires a hands-on experience of GlobalTechy's way of life. The event, held in a repurposed warehouse decorated with makeshift totems made from reclaimed office supplies, featured a series of team-building exercises that parodied traditional tribal initiation rituals. New employees were asked to complete a treasure hunt that involved deciphering clues hidden in meticulously written emails and navigating a labyrinth of cubicles - each checkpoint marked by a different corporate buzzword. The day, intended to foster unity, ended up becoming a festival of irreverent humour as participants began to mock the very idea of a forced cultural narrative. Laughter echoed down the aisles as even the most senior managers found themselves swept up in the absurdity of it all, temporarily shedding the weight of formal decorum in favor of light-hearted camaraderie.

In quieter moments, when the hum of fluorescent lights mingled with the soft tapping of keyboards, the subtle rituals of GlobalTechy continued unabated. There was a sacred unspoken rule about the precise moment to check one's email - neither too early to seem overeager nor too late to risk being branded as detached. There were also the legendary unwritten policies of the breakroom, where debates about the proper waiting time before repairing a malfunctioning coffee machine could inadvertently turn into spirited discussions on the nature of modern labour. These everyday interactions, though seemingly trivial on their own, wove together to form the rich tapestry of corporate culture - a tapestry that, like the intricate patterns found on ancient pottery, told the story of a community's hopes, fears, and shared sense of identity.

And so, as GlobalTechy pressed ever onward into the uncertain future, its employees continued to navigate a delicate dance between tradition and transformation. The high-flying announcements of strategic pivots and quarterly goals provided a stark backdrop to the deep-seated, almost instinctual behaviours that had long defined human interaction. Whether it was through the subtle mimicry of leadership language, the ritualistic nods during meetings filled with jargon, or the sly jokes exchanged behind closed doors, the culture of the organisation remained both a source of pride and a revelatory force - a living, breathing example of how humanity, with all its quirks and contradictions, always found a way to adapt.

Maria, now deeply entrenched in the fabric of GlobalTechy, had unraveled the core mystery of corporate culture: it was not something imposed from above like an edict written in stone, but an emergent phenomenon – a constantly evolving blend of individual quirks, shared narratives, and enduring human rituals. Her work, bridging anthropology and modern business, became a beacon of insight in an age where the line between human intuition and mechanistic precision was increasingly blurred. She wrote of how leadership, much like the tribal elders of yore, played double roles as both the architects and the frontline performers of culture. They crafted the ceremonial language and then, with a knowing smile, watched as their words were repeated ad infinitum – a loop of synergy, alignment, and innovation that, ironically, often defied precise definition.

In a final, reflective gathering – one that would be immortalized in the annals of GlobalTechy lore – Richard called the entire workforce together for an all-hands meeting of extravagant proportions. The room, packed to the brim with employees from every corner of the organization, brimmed with an expectant energy that bordered on the sacred. Richard took center stage, his charismatic aura accentuated by the soft glow of stage lights and the hum of anticipatory murmurs. With the solemnity of a high priest delivering a benediction, he repeated the rallying cry of the organization: "Our culture is what defines us!" The words reverberated around the room, mingling with the subtle, unspoken laughter of an audience that had long learned to appreciate the delicious irony embedded in every utterance.

As the meeting drew to a close, whispers of amusement and secret smiles were exchanged among the employees. For they knew, beyond the formal mottoes and glittering presentations, that the true essence of GlobalTechy's culture was something enigmatic – a mosaic of the old and the new, of ancient human instincts and modern technological wonders. It was a culture that had survived and thrived not because it was imposed, but because it had been allowed to evolve organically – through countless interactions, quiet acts of subversion, and yes, even moments of spontaneous humour.

Thus, the story of GlobalTechy Enterprises continued to unfold, page by page, in an epic saga that bridged the gap between the primordial and the futuristic. Its halls, filled with both high-tech marvels and age-old rituals, served as a living museum of modern culture – a testament to the fact that, no matter how advanced our technologies become, the heart of any community is eternally rooted in the human need to belong, to express, and to remember that beneath every official pronouncement, there lies a secret narrative only the observant can decipher.

And so, in that grand labyrinth of cubicles and boardrooms, where AI-generated memos and human laughter intertwined like threads in a timeless tapestry, the invisible force of corporate culture reigned supreme. It was a force that shaped every interaction, guided every decision, and turned everyday office life into a modern-day epic – a story as humorous as it was profound, as mundane as it was mystical. In the end, GlobalTechy was more than just a multinational corporation; it was a vibrant, ever-changing society, a living experiment in the evolution of culture where the echoes of ancient tribal rituals met the relentless march of the digital age.

In recounting this grand and oddly entertaining saga, one cannot help but marvel at the unyielding spirit of human creativity and its uncanny ability to infuse meaning into even the most mechanical of settings. The story of GlobalTechy, from its meticulously planned retreats to its spontaneous moments of irony, serves as a reminder that culture - whether etched on cave walls or encoded in algorithms - is ultimately about the shared experiences, the silent conspiracies, and the subtle rebellions that define us as social beings. It is a narrative that endures, ever adapting to the rhythms of time, and always leaves room for one last, knowing smile in the corridors after the boss has finally left the room.

Thus, as Maria closed the final chapter of her manuscript and gazed out at the endless stream of employees hustling through the halls of GlobalTechy, she felt a deep sense of connection to both the past and the present - a feeling that transcended boardroom battles and digital dogmas. Here, in this extraordinary fusion of ancient wisdom and modern enterprise, lay the eternal truth: that culture, in all its wondrous complexity, is not something that can be manufactured in a boardroom. Rather, it is a living, breathing saga - one that continues to be written by each and every one of us, in our daily acts of survival, rebellion, creativity, and laughter.

And so, the legend of GlobalTechy Enterprises endures - a grand, sprawling epic woven from the threads of human history and powered by the relentless, paradoxical engine of modern technology. It is a story that reminds us that in the dance between human intuition and algorithmic precision, in the interplay of tradition and innovation, we find not only the spirit of a company, but the timeless, vibrant pulse of *humanity* itself.

IV

The Path Forward – Leadership in Action

10

The EU's New AI Act: Leading the AI Regulation

The future of artificial intelligence is being shaped not solely by engineers and coders but by visionary policymakers and leaders determined to steer its development in the right direction. No longer is AI the exclusive domain of isolated research laboratories or the guarded strategic plans of Silicon Valley giants. Instead, it has emerged as a central pillar of global policy - a field where leadership is not an abstract ideal but a concrete, driving force that determines the digital age. Nowhere is this more evident than in the European Union, where policymakers and lawmakers in the European Parliament are actively crafting the policy frameworks that will chart the future of AI and, by extension, digital society.

In March 2024, the European Parliament marked a watershed moment by enacting the EU AI Act, a comprehensive regulation designed to impose a structured and principled approach to AI governance. This legislation, the result of years of persistent debate, rigorous consultations, and intricate legislative processes, did more than merely set down rules; it solidified the EU's reputation as a global rule-maker in the digital space – a mantle previously worn with distinction through efforts like the General Data Protection Regulation (GDPR). However, it is crucial to understand that laws of this magnitude do not arise in isolation. They are the fruit of vision, resilience, and, fundamentally, leadership that dares to balance innovation with accountability.

The journey toward the EU AI Act began long before the final vote in the plenary chamber of the European Parliament. A sprawling network of voices - comprising members of parliament (MEPs), expert committees, industry representatives, civil society organizations, and think tanks - engaged in continuous dialogue, underscoring the urgency of regulating AI. This process was not a simple matter of technical adjustments or bureaucratic reshuffling; it was a demonstration of leadership at its finest. The European Parliament had to grapple with profound questions: How should we balance the benefits of rapid technological progress against the need to protect individual rights? What ethical principles should guide the development of AI systems that touch every facet of society? And how can policymakers ensure that regulation does not stifle innovation but encourages responsible technological advancement?

In this context, the story of the EU AI Act becomes one of transformational leadership. The leaders who championed its passage recognized early on that artificial intelligence is not merely a technological challenge but a societal one that intersects with ethical, economic, and environmental dimensions. They understood that AI holds the promise of driving unprecedented economic growth and societal progress while also being capable of entrenching biases, eroding privacy, and undermining democratic institutions if left unchecked. It was this dual nature of AI - a force both empowering and disruptive - that compelled these leaders to adopt an approach based on precaution, foresight, and a steadfast commitment to human dignity.

Behind the polished rhetoric in the corridors of the European Parliament, a complex machinery of legislative processes was at work. Any law within the EU, particularly one as transformative as the AI Act, must first navigate a maze of institutions designed to ensure democratic accountability, expert input, and cross-national consensus. The European Commission, with its agenda-setting power and technical expertise, initially drafted proposals that reflected a synthesis of technological realities and ethical aspirations. Drawing on extensive consultations with stakeholders from academia, industry, and society at large, the Commission's proposals laid down broad strategic goals.

But it was in the heart of the European Parliament that these technical proposals would be extensively scrutinised, debated, and refined. Unlike in many parts of the world where technological innovation is often left to market mechanisms, the EU's legislative process is marked by a deep commitment to participatory democracy. Committees such as the Committee on Industry, Research and Energy (ITRE) and the Committee on Civil Liberties, Justice and Home Affairs (LIBE) played pivotal roles in shaping the Act. These committees, composed of MEPs with expertise in technology, ethics, and public policy, meticulously examined every clause, insisted on transparent consultations, and ensured that the regulation would not only promote innovation but would safeguard fundamental rights.

In several marathon sessions that often extended late into the night, parliamentary leaders brokered compromises between divergent views. On one side were proponents of stringent regulation, arguing that the rapid evolution of AI technologies had outpaced existing legal frameworks and posed a real threat to privacy and social justice. On the other side were voices cautioning against over-regulation, warning that an overly restrictive regime might hamper economic competitiveness and slow down the pace of beneficial technological innovations. In balancing these perspectives, EU leaders showcased an extraordinary mastery of negotiation, an ability to parse nuanced technical details while keeping sight of long-term societal goals.

It is important to note that leadership in this arena goes far beyond a simple dictatorial imposition of rules. Rather, it involves a delicate orchestration of power, expertise, and diplomatic acumen. Leaders in the European Parliament did not view the AI Act as a static document; they saw it as a living framework that would evolve with technological advances and emerging ethical challenges. As such, provisions for periodic review and adaptation were built into the legislation, ensuring that it could remain relevant in an ever-changing digital landscape. Such foresight underlines a critical aspect of leadership - anticipating future challenges and being prepared to recalibrate policy measures in response.

Beyond the immediate legislative process, the EU AI Act has had a broader geopolitical impact. Thanks to what is informally known as the Brussels Effect, decisions made within the walls of the European Parliament reverberate well beyond Europe's borders. Multinational companies and policymakers around the globe now find themselves compelled to take note of the stringent standards devised in Brussels. For those wishing to operate within the EU market or to interface with European digital infrastructures, compliance with the AI Act's provisions is not optional but essential. This extraterritorial influence underscores how leadership, when enacted properly, can serve as a catalyst for global regulatory harmonisation, compelling nations as far afield as Washington, Beijing, and Tokyo to revisit their own policy frameworks.

Yet, the multifaceted nature of leadership in AI governance means that the EU's approach has often stood in stark contrast to other global models. For instance, while the United States has long embraced a relatively laissez-faire stance - preferring industry self-regulation and market-driven evolution - the EU has taken a more precautionary stance. American policymakers, particularly under the Biden administration, have introduced voluntary guidelines and commitments from tech giants, emphasising economic dynamism and innovation growth. However, they have refrained from adopting the comprehensive legislative framework that the EU has championed. While this divergent approach reflects differing national priorities and cultural attitudes toward regulation, it also highlights a central theme: leadership in the field of AI is as much about values as it is about technical solutions.

In the case of China, the landscape is strikingly different once more. Chinese policy on AI is deeply intertwined with state objectives and national security imperatives. The Chinese government has invested heavily in AI research and has enacted strict regulations that not only govern technological development but also serve the broader goal of digital authoritarianism. Here, leadership is not premised on an open, democratic dialogue but on a top-down approach to control and enforcement. While China's model may achieve rapid advances and offer a stark contrast in regulatory philosophy, it raises critical questions about the balance between state interests and individual freedoms - questions that sit at the very heart of the EU's legislative debates.

At its core, the EU's leadership in AI regulation is about trust. Trust that citizens' data will be protected, trust that automated systems will operate fairly, and trust that decisions affecting billions of lives will be made with the utmost integrity and careful deliberation. Building such trust requires leaders who are not only skilled in the technical dimensions of AI - understanding its algorithms, data dependencies, and infrastructural requirements - but who also possess a profound ethical sensibility. EU policymakers committed to the AI Act have repeatedly demonstrated that effective governance is not a mere exercise in legal formality; it is a commitment to an ethical vision of technology that serves the common good.

This ethical vision is underpinned by the traditional philosophical debates about the purpose of technology in society. Drawing on the insights of ancient thinkers like Aristotle, many EU leaders have argued that AI should not be aimed solely at enhancing efficiency or maximising profits. Rather, in the spirit of eudaimonia - the notion that the highest human good is a life of flourishing - AI should be deployed to promote societal well-being, ensure human dignity, and improve the quality of life for all citizens. This philosophical grounding transforms the legislative process from a technical exercise into a moral mission, one where laws are seen as instruments for fostering a more equitable and humane digital future.

The transformation of debate into legislation within the EU is emblematic of the broader challenges faced by societies globally. In every corner of the legislative arena, there is an underlying tension between progress and prudence, between the need to capitalise on technological advancements and the imperative to protect the vulnerable from unintended consequences. In the rich tapestry of the EU legislative process, leadership is showcased in every debate, every amendment proposed, every compromise struck between various interest groups. Each decision, each parliamentary vote, represents a commitment to ensuring that the promise of AI does not come at the expense of democratic accountability and public trust.

One cannot overstate the role of corporate leadership in this ecosystem. The rapid technological strides made by tech giants such as OpenAI, Google DeepMind, and Microsoft have thrust them into positions of significant influence over the development and implementation of AI systems. While these companies drive innovation on the ground, their decisions regarding transparency, safety protocols, and deployment strategies also affect regulatory outcomes. Thus, there is a dynamic interplay between corporate decision-making and government regulation. The EU, aware of this interplay, has insisted that the AI Act be complemented by rigorous mechanisms for oversight and accountability, ensuring that private enterprise does not undermine public interest.

The process of legislating the AI Act within the EU is emblematic of an enduring commitment to open dialogue and multilateral cooperation. In the preparatory phases, numerous public consultations were organized, inviting input from diverse stakeholders - including academics, industry experts, civil society advocates, and ordinary citizens. These consultations went beyond formal hearings; they were structured as participatory workshops and roundtable discussions. The

European Parliament's Office for Citizens' Rights ensured that even the voices of individuals from marginalised communities were heard, ensuring that the final text of the Act would reflect a balanced perspective. This process not only enriched the lawmaking experience but also fostered a sense of collective ownership over the final product. Leadership, in this instance, was not concentrated in a handful of bureaucrats or politicians; it was dispersed across a vast network of engaged citizens and experts, each contributing to a shared vision of ethical AI governance.

Furthermore, the legislative journey was not without its challenges. Debate over the precise definitions of "high-risk" AI applications, discussions on the thresholds for human intervention, and disputes over liability in cases of AI malfunctions were all subjects of heated contention. Each of these debates required a nuanced understanding of both the technology and its broader societal implications. The seasoned MEPs, many of whom had served through previous transformative legislative battles such as those surrounding data protection, leveraged their experience to build bridges across ideological divides. They demonstrated that leadership in the age of AI is not characterised by rigidity or dogmatism but by the willingness to engage with complexity, listen to opposing views, and craft policies that are both flexible and forward-looking.

At the heart of this legislative process lies the European Parliament - a unique institution that embodies the democratic spirit of the EU. Composed of elected representatives from across member states, the Parliament is both a forum for debate and a battleground for competing visions of Europe's digital future. Here, leadership is exercised in every committee meeting and plenary session, where decisions are reached not through unilateral imposition but through consensus-building and rigorous debate. This collaborative ethos is what has allowed the EU to emerge as a global leader in digital regulation. The very structure of the Parliament - its committees, its plenaries, its built-in mechanisms for cross-party dialogue - ensures that policies like the AI Act are the product of collective wisdom and that every regulatory measure is rooted in a broad-based democratic mandate.

It is also worth noting that the leadership demonstrated in the development of the AI Act reflects a broader strategic shift within the EU. Over the past decade, the Union has made it clear that it aims not only to be a market for digital products but also a shaper of global technological norms. The AI Act is a bold step in that direction, signaling to the world that the EU intends to set the rules for the future of technology. By proactively addressing the risks and opportunities presented by AI, EU leaders are taking control of a narrative that many hoped would be dominated by commercial interests and technological determinism. Instead, they are crafting a story where technology is harnessed in the service of democracy, human rights, and sustainable development.

Moreover, the leadership required to shepherd the AI Act to fruition is emblematic of a larger vision of what European leadership should entail. It is not enough to simply react to emerging technologies; the leaders of tomorrow must anticipate the changes that AI and other digital innovations will usher in and prepare society accordingly. This forward-thinking approach extends beyond regulatory details to broader questions of workforce transformation, educational, and societal resilience in the face of rapid technological change. In this sense, the legislative process behind the AI Act can be seen as a microcosm of a larger, ongoing journey toward a more adaptive, responsive, and ethically grounded form of governance.

Environmental considerations further complicate the landscape of AI regulation, and here too, EU leaders have taken a stand. As data centers and high-performance computing platforms consume vast amounts of energy, questions about the sustainability of AI become ever more pressing. In parallel with discussions on privacy and ethics, the AI Act also contains provisions aimed at encouraging energy-efficient practices and reducing the carbon footprint of digital infrastructure. This intersection of technological advancement and environmental stewardship encapsulates a central tenet of EU leadership: that progress must not come at the cost of planetary health. Integrating energy considerations into AI regulation is a testament to the vision of European policymakers who see technology not in isolation but as an integral part of a sustainable future.

Corporate responsibility, too, features prominently in this narrative of leadership. While the AI Act imposes obligations on private entities, it also underscores an important principle: with power comes responsibility. Tech CEOs and corporate leaders find themselves at the nexus of innovation and accountability. Their decisions on how to implement AI systems, ensure transparency, and safeguard data privacy are as consequential as the laws passed in parliaments. In many debates leading up to the Act's adoption, corporate voices argued for more flexible, market-friendly solutions. However, the overarching consensus among EU leaders was that without robust regulatory guardrails, the promise of AI could quickly turn into a perilous gamble. This stance - firm yet open to dialogue - exemplifies what it means to lead in a complex era where private and public interests must be carefully balanced.

In reflecting on the formulation and passage of the AI Act, one is reminded of timeless philosophical wisdom. Aristotle's concept of eudaimonia, with its emphasis on human flourishing as the ultimate goal, provides an apt framework for understanding the aspirations behind the legislation. AI should not be seen merely as an engine of efficiency or a profit-maximizing tool, but as a technology that should enhance the human condition. Similarly, the cautionary notes of Plato about the dangers of unchecked power and unaccountable rulers resonate today, reminding us that automated decision-making must always remain subject to human oversight and ethical scrutiny. Kant's insistence on moral duty ties neatly into this discussion by framing ethical AI as not only a preventive measure against harm but also as a proactive commitment to the common good.

The legislative history of the AI Act also highlights the importance of international collaboration. The EU's robust debates and procedural safeguards have been closely watched by other regions, prompting discussions on the future of AI regulation worldwide. The Brussels Effect is not merely an economic phenomenon but also a diplomatic one, as decisions made within the EU often set benchmarks for global regulatory standards. Policymakers in continents far removed from Europe's political arena, from Asia to the Americas, now face the imperative of harmonizing with the high standards set by their European counterparts. In this scenario, leadership is not insular but interconnected - European leadership serves as a beacon, prompting a cooperative spirit that transcends national boundaries.

Yet even as the AI Act signals a bold vision for the future, leaders in Europe are acutely aware of the potential pitfalls. The rapid pace of technological change means that no regulation can be entirely foolproof. AI systems evolve, new applications emerge, and unforeseen challenges inevitably arise. Leadership, therefore, must be both proactive and reactive - establishing frameworks that are robust enough to guide current developments while also being agile enough to adapt to new realities. This dual mandate requires a deep understanding of technology, economics, and sociology, along with a sincere willingness to engage with all stakeholders across society.

The mosaic of expertise and perspectives that contributed to the AI Act reflects in part the EU's commitment to multilateralism. Every voice, from technologists working on cutting-edge algorithms to ethicists and social scientists examining the societal impacts, found a place in the debate. Such inclusivity is a hallmark of leadership that is not confined to power or prestige but is defined by the capacity to listen, learn, and integrate diverse forms of knowledge. In the hallowed halls of the European Parliament, where debates can sometimes stretch over weeks or months, this commitment to thorough deliberation underscores a profound respect for democratic processes and a deep-seated belief that effective governance can only arise from broad consensus.

For many, the passage of the EU AI Act stands as a definitive moment - a turning point when the digital future was no longer left solely to technologists and market forces, but was actively sculpted by leaders determined to make technology work for everyone. It is an enduring testament to the transformative potential of leadership that is willing to grapple with complexity, to balance competing priorities with both rigor and compassion, and to envision a future where technology enriches human life without compromising core values.

In summing up this journey, one might note that the legislative process behind the AI Act is as much about *forging a shared vision* as it is about enacting policy. EU leadership in AI regulation exemplifies a proactive strategy that places human rights, environmental sustainability, and ethical imperatives at the center of technological progress. It is a model of governance that many around the globe now aspire to, even as they adapt it to their own political cultures and circumstances.

The story of the EU AI Act reminds us that leadership in the digital era transcends the narrow confines of technical expertise. It demands an integrative approach whereby lawmakers, technologists, environmentalists, and philosophers come together to chart a course for the common good. In every debate, every committee meeting, and every negotiated compromise, the underlying message was clear: the future of AI - and indeed, the future of society - will be determined not merely by the algorithms we create, but by the values we embed within them.

As Europe stands at the forefront of this global dialogue, its leadership is a telling reflection of the vision it holds for the future. A future where regulation does not stifle innovation but channels it for social benefit; a future where accountability, transparency, and ethical grounding are as much a part of technological progress as economic growth; and a future where every citizen can trust that the digital tools transforming their lives are guided by a humane and visionary spirit.

Today, as nations worldwide continue to wrestle with similar challenges, the EU's approach serves as a paragon of what is possible when leadership is informed by both courage and compassion. The legislative journey of the AI Act is a story that will be studied and emulated for decades to come – a story of how a collective commitment to responsible innovation can reshape not only policy but the very future of human progress. In this brave new world, leadership is both the compass and the map, charting a course toward a future where technology and ethics walk hand in hand, guiding humanity into a digital age defined not by surveillance and control, but by freedom, dignity, and opportunity for all.

Looking forward, the EU and its Parliament continue to recognise that while the AI Act marks a significant milestone, it is but one chapter in the ongoing dialogue on digital governance. As new challenges emerge – be they related to the integration of AI in healthcare, education, transportation, or security – the need for responsive, forward-thinking leadership remains paramount. The legislative process, with its layered intricacies and deep democratic roots, provides a robust framework for addressing these issues, ensuring that every decision made today contributes to a sustainable and inclusive tomorrow.

In our rapidly evolving world, the EU's leadership on AI regulation offers an inspiring template: one that harmonises innovation with responsibility, progress with preservation, and technological dynamism with ethical integrity. It offers hope that, with the right vision and steadfast commitment, the digital future will be one in which every citizen is empowered, every innovation is harnessed for the common good, and every leap forward is taken with a profound respect for the human spirit.

Ultimately, as European leaders have demonstrated through the passage of the AI Act, the future of AI – and by extension, the future of society – is not predetermined by market forces or technological trends. It is actively constructed by the choices of those in power, the deliberations of elected representatives, and the collective wisdom of a society that chooses to put people before profit. In doing so, they do not merely regulate technology; they define the very essence of leadership in the digital age.

By embracing a vision that is as principled as it is progressive, the EU has set forth a blueprint for the world. It is a blueprint that recognises the transformative potential of AI while remaining ever mindful of the ethical, social, and environmental challenges that accompany this new frontier. As the European Parliament and its dedicated legislators continue to lead the charge against the uncertainties of tomorrow, their work remains a shining example of how leadership, when infused with conviction, integrity, and a genuine concern for the common good, can reshape not only policy but the very future of our global community.

11

Toward Net Zero and Beyond

In our contemporary global landscape, the imperative to achieve net zero emissions has blossomed into much more than an environmental target - it has become a symbol of our collective responsibility to one another and the legacy we leave for future generations. As we close this book, we find ourselves at a critical juncture where the challenge of climate change intersects with our deepest ethical and philosophical considerations. The net zero goal is not solely about the reduction of greenhouse gases; it is a clarion call to care for one another, to reimagine the fabric of our societies, and to embrace leadership that is compassionate, visionary, and inclusive.

Emerging economies, still engaged in the strenuous battle against poverty and navigating the often tumultuous waters of rapid industrialisation, have traditionally perceived stringent carbon pricing as an unwelcome imposition - a potentially stifling constraint on their development. These nations face the dual challenge of striving for economic progress while being asked to shoulder the burdens of a global environmental crisis. Yet within this tension lies an opportunity: the chance to harmonise economic advancement with sustainable practices, fostering a future where development and environmental stewardship are not mutually exclusive but intrinsically linked.

At the heart of this pursuit is leadership - a concept that transcends the mere allocation of authority and policy-making. True leadership in the context of net zero is defined by its capacity to inspire empathy and a sense of shared responsibility. It invites a profound re-evaluation of what we mean by progress and success. It demands that political leaders not only articulate policies that target carbon reduction but also weave a broader narrative that celebrates mutual care, societal cohesion, and the moral imperative to leave behind a world that is healthier, more just, and more resilient.

Political leaders, by virtue of their positions, possess the unique ability to forge alliances, galvanise communities, and, most importantly, to articulate a vision that transcends narrow national or partisan interests. In their hands lies the power to transform the global response to climate change from a series of isolated policy mandates into a concerted, collaborative movement - a shared journey towards a sustainable future. It is this transformative leadership that the net zero imperative demands. Rather than relying solely on coercion or economic levies, political leaders must engage deeply with the ideals of caring and solidarity. They must recognise that policies on carbon emissions are intertwined with issues such as social justice, equity, and the fundamental right to a liveable planet.

Throughout this book, we have delved into myriad facets of our contemporary existence - from the interplay of technology and tradition to the balance between economic progress and environmental decay. The philosophy underpinning these diverse discussions has steadily reinforced one salient truth: that our destinies are inexorably interlinked. Whether it is the impact of climate change on the world's poorest communities, or the ethical dilemmas posed by rapidly advancing automation, a recurring theme has emerged. That theme is the undeniable need to care for one another - not just the familiar faces of our communities but also the unseen, the marginalised, and those whose voices are often drowned in the cacophony of global markets and political opportunism.

The net zero imperative offers a powerful framework for reimagining this interconnectedness. In essence, to pursue net zero is to engage in a process of deep systemic transformation - restructuring our economic systems, reorienting our societal values, and rebalancing the relationship we have with our environment. The environmental challenge, in this light, is as much a socio-political quest as it is scientific. It calls for a leadership that is not constrained by traditional boundaries, one that recognises the intrinsic value of every human life and every natural ecosystem.

This new form of leadership is distinguished by its inherent empathy. It embodies an understanding that policies which might appear economically challenging in the short term can - and must - be balanced by a broader commitment to social welfare. Leaders must earn the trust and confidence of the people they serve by demonstrating that the journey to net zero is not a sacrifice but a transformation: one that improves the quality of life for all, fosters innovation, and paves the way for a more equitable distribution of resources. In countries still battling poverty and striving for industrial progress, this means constructing policies that blend environmental sustainability with economic opportunity - ensuring that no community is left behind as we transition to a greener future.

Philosophically, we are called, at this moment, to reassess the way we view success and progress. The utilitarian calculus of the past - where economic growth was often measured solely by gross domestic product - must be replaced by a more nuanced indicator that honours well-being, ecological balance, and social equity. In the broader intellectual discourse explored in earlier chapters, we argued that sustainable development is not merely an economic necessity but a moral obligation. Leaders must, therefore, navigate the delicate interplay between immediate human needs and the long-term welfare of the planet. This duality is central to the challenge at hand: reconciling harsh economic realities with the soft ethics of care and mutual responsibility.

One cannot discuss the role of political leadership in achieving net zero without acknowledging the considerable scepticism and resistance derived from fears about economic loss and disruption. However, history tells us that transformative change is often met with resistance before its benefits are fully realised. True leaders recognise that the transition to a sustainable economy will require not only structural adjustments but also a cultural shift - a reorientation towards recognising that modern prosperity should not come at the expense of the planet or the vulnerable. It is in this context that political leaders must emerge not as commanders enforcing draconian measures, but as compassionate stewards guiding us through uncharted territory, one that harmonises economic resilience with environmental urgency.

The process of forging the international consensus needed to achieve net zero is inherently complex. It is reminiscent of the multinational efforts taken during critical global moments

– when nations, despite their differences, came together to confront a common challenge. The global response to the climate crisis must be as inclusive as it is transformative. Leaders are called not merely to negotiate treaties and sign accords, but to nurture a global ethos of responsibility, akin to the shared commitment of citizens to look after one another. This is the philosophical heart of our discourse – a commitment that, in striving for net zero, we are also striving to build an international community where each nation's interests are balanced by a regard for global fairness and mutual well-being.

Moreover, the net zero challenge compels us to address the ethical dimensions of our global economic structure. The traditional story of development has been one of accumulation and expansion, often achieved at unsustainable costs to the environment and to the future. This book has long argued that the model of endless growth is fundamentally at odds with the finite nature of our ecological systems. A sustainable future demands a reorientation – a rebalancing of our metrics of success towards those that value renewal and resilience over exploitation and excess. Political leaders, therefore, must pioneer a new era of economic thought, one where investment in green technologies and sustainable practices is not seen as a burden but as an opportunity – a chance to lead the world in innovation while rectifying past imbalances.

In practical terms, this transformation calls for a concerted effort to redesign our policies and economic structures. It requires investing in renewable energy, fostering circular economies, and creating social safety nets that cushion those affected by the inevitable upheavals of the transition. Emerging economies, in particular, must be supported through tailored financial mechanisms, technology transfers, and capacity-building initiatives. Only through a considerate and empathetic approach can political leaders ensure that the perceived burden of net zero is transformed into an engine of global prosperity and collective well-being.

As we examine these challenges through a philosophical lens, it becomes clear that the journey to net zero demands us to confront fundamental questions about the meaning of progress. Is the wealth of a nation measured solely by its industrial output, or should it be gauged by the extent to which it nurtures the lives of its citizens and the health of its environment? The net zero imperative urges us to broaden our perspective, recognising that caring for each other lies at the core of sustainable development. Political leaders must thus engage in ethical reasoning, bringing to the fore principles of fairness, responsibility, and the intrinsic value of each human life.

This ethical dimension is woven throughout the chapter's narrative - the idea that achieving net zero is not just an environmental challenge but a moral mandate. It compels us to live with a sensitivity that transcends utilitarian benefits and addresses the core of what it means to be human: to care, to empathise, and to act for the common good. The stakes are profound. Without a principled commitment to these values, political leaders may find themselves advocating for policies that, while technically sound in reducing emissions, fail to reckon with the deep-seated inequalities and social challenges that plague our global community.

As we reach the end of this book, it becomes apparent that our struggle for net zero is a mirror reflecting all our aspirations and anxieties. The political landscape is replete with uncertainties, from the volatile dynamics of international relations to the internal pressures within nations still grappling with inequality. Against this backdrop, the journey towards net zero must be framed not as an isolated technical challenge, but as an overarching narrative of care and responsibility – a narrative that summons us to redefine leadership itself.

Political leaders today stand at a crossroads. On one hand, they are expected to manage short-term crises – economic downturns, political instability, and immediate public health concerns. On the other hand, they are tasked with steering the long-term destiny of nations in a world destabilised by climate change. It is a dual responsibility that demands both immediate action and visionary planning. The profound changes required to reach net zero will demand a delicate balance between addressing pressing demographic and economic woes and planting the seeds for a sustainable future. Leaders must therefore be capable of articulating a comprehensive vision – a vision that integrates policies for economic rejuvenation with those for environmental restoration.

This vision must also entail a significant degree of political courage. The path to net zero is fraught with sacrifices and difficult trade-offs. Political leaders must be prepared to challenge entrenched interests and overcome resistance from those reticent to change an established economic order. They must be willing to invest in new technologies and green infrastructure, even in the face of criticism or short-term economic setbacks. Ultimately, the success of these endeavours hinges on a leadership that is not only adept at navigating immediate crises but also at inspiring long-term hope and resilience.

The lessons of history remind us that the most significant transformations are rarely instantaneous. Instead, they are the result of persistent effort, progressive vision, and an unwavering commitment to the common good. Political leaders must therefore harness the best of human ingenuity and compassion to forge a path towards net zero, one that is inclusive, participatory, and deeply humane. They must work alongside international organisations, grassroots movements, and the private sector, recognising that the challenges posed by climate change transcend the capacities of any single nation or institution.

In reflecting on the ideas developed earlier in this book, it is essential to reaffirm that the environmental crisis is a manifestation of deeper, systemic issues - issues related to power, inequality, and the legacy of colonial exploitation. The net zero imperative asks us to address not only the emissions that poison our atmosphere, but also the social and economic structures that have brought us to this precipice. As such, the role of political leaders becomes multifaceted: they must not only push for green policies but also strive to dismantle the unequal systems that exacerbate vulnerability and hinder progress.

This multifaceted leadership should be rooted in the recognition that caring for the planet and caring for each other are inextricably linked. The vulnerabilities exposed by climate change - whether in the form of natural disasters, food insecurity, or mass migrations - are a stark reminder that no community exists in isolation. Political leaders must thus foster policies that are as empathetic as they are efficient, as innovative as they are inclusive. They must champion a vision in which every person, regardless of their socio-economic status, is afforded the opportunity to contribute to and benefit from a sustainable future.

In the final analysis, the journey to net zero is a journey towards redefining what it means to be human in a rapidly changing world. It requires a paradigm shift – a fundamental transformation in our relationship with nature, with each other, and with the very concept of progress. As we close the pages of this book, what emerges is a call to reimagine leadership itself. Leadership that once revolved around control and authority must now pivot towards engagement and empathy. It is a call to recognise that true power lies in the ability to care, to listen, and to act with both courage and compassion.

The philosophical reflections scattered throughout our discussions have consistently pointed towards an ethical awakening. This awakening is a reminder that every action we take has repercussions that extend far beyond the immediate moment. The path to net zero is emblematic of that truth – it is a transformation that carries within it the promise of not just a healthier planet, but of deeper human connections. It speaks to the heart of what it means to collectively shoulder responsibility for the future of our world, and, in doing so, to affirm the dignity and rights of every human being.

As we look towards a future that is inherently uncertain, political leadership becomes the nexus where vision meets reality. In this era of profound change, leaders are no longer merely custodians of state power; they are architects of a shared destiny. They are tasked with the monumental challenge of crafting policies that are economically viable, environmentally sound, and socially just – all while fostering a global narrative of hope and communal care. The transformation required is not just technical or economic; it is fundamentally moral. It commands that we reflect on our values, renegotiate our priorities, and ultimately, reaffirm our commitment to each other.

In sum, the convergence of the net zero imperative with the principles of caring and compassionate leadership represents the very essence of our future. As we close this book, let us remember that the journey to net zero is not a solitary expedition but a communal pilgrimage – a journey that necessitates every hand, every voice, and every heart to beat in unison for the common good. Political leaders, as well as citizens, are called upon to embrace this challenge with a spirit of resilience and an unwavering belief that a more sustainable, equitable, and prosperous future is within our grasp.

Our actions today will sculpt the world of tomorrow. By championing policies that nurture both our natural environment and our social bonds, by fostering an ethos of care that transcends national borders and economic disparities, and by embracing a leadership model that is as visionary as it is empathetic, we can forge a path that not only achieves net zero emissions but also honours the timeless imperative to care for one another. This is the legacy we must build – a legacy rooted in the conviction that the well-being of our planet and its inhabitants is the highest good, and that our collective success depends on the compassion and unity that define our shared humanity.

As political leaders rise to this challenge, let them be guided by the enduring truths explored throughout this book. Let their policies be imbued with both moral clarity and pragmatic wisdom. And let us, as a global community, recognise that the journey to net zero is a profound act of solidarity – a testament to our ability to transcend differences, to overcome obstacles, and to build a future characterized by justice, sustainability, and care. In the final reckoning, the net zero imperative is not merely about carbon emissions; it is about reshaping the world into one where every person is valued, every community is supported, and every act of leadership is an investment in the future of us all.

Thus, as we draw this discourse to a close, we are left with a resounding truth: the path to net zero is a path of care, leadership, and shared responsibility. It beckons us not to retreat into isolation, but to unite under a banner of collective purpose. Political leaders at every level – local, national, and international – must answer this call. Their vision, their empathy, and their commitment to justice will determine whether we can move beyond the challenges of today and into a tomorrow that is brighter, fairer, and sustainable.

In the twilight of our discussion, let it be known that the journey towards net zero is as much an ethical quest as it is an environmental mandate. It is a journey that reminds us that caring for the planet is inherently intertwined with caring for each other. It reaffirms that in a world beset by climate change, economic inequality, and social disintegration, the true strength of our leadership lies in its ability to unite – to inspire the best in humanity, to empower those in need, and to build institutions that reflect the highest ideals of human endeavour.

Looking back on all the ideas laid out in this book – from the analysis of economic paradigms and political dynamics to the philosophical meditations on justice and responsibility – we find that they converge in a single, transformative vision. A vision where environmental sustainability and human solidarity are not at odds but are mutually reinforcing. A vision that calls for political leaders to lead with not only their intellect and authority but also with their hearts. A vision that transforms the daunting challenges of our age into stepping stones towards a future where net zero is not the end goal, but the foundation upon which a thriving, inclusive society is built.

In this final chapter, as the narrative of our shared journey comes to a close, we are reminded that the future is ours to shape. It is a future where every decision, every policy, and every act of leadership is an affirmation of our commitment to one another. A future where caring for the environment is synonymous with caring for our communities, where sustainable development is the measure of progress, and where the net zero imperative serves as a beacon guiding us towards a more compassionate and just world.

May we all, leaders and citizens alike, draw inspiration from the challenges we face, and may we approach the monumental task of reimagining our world with a spirit of collaboration, empathy, and undying hope. The endeavour to achieve net zero is not merely a technical adjustment or an economic strategy - it is a profound statement of our values, a declaration that our collective future will be one defined by care, inclusivity, and the relentless pursuit of justice.

In closing, let this be a testament to the power of unified, compassionate leadership. Let it serve as a reminder that in the quest for a sustainable future, every voice matters, every act of care is significant, and every leader has a critical role to play. The journey to net zero is our shared responsibility, our common challenge, and, ultimately, our greatest opportunity to create a world that honours the best of who we are.

Epilogue

As I complete this book, the world's political landscape seems to drift further from the principles of true leadership. In one of the world's most influential democracies, dark rhetoric drowns out reason, diplomacy is cast aside, and those entrusted with power serve not the people, but a figure elevated beyond question. Integrity is no longer a virtue but an inconvenience, and authoritarianism is met not with resistance, but with reward.

How, then, can we still speak of leadership, integrity, and service? Because true leadership is not defined by those who betray it, but by those who uphold it against all odds. It is found in those who refuse to surrender their principles, who challenge deception with truth, and who understand that power is a duty, not a privilege.

History does not remember the sycophants – it remembers those who stood firm when it mattered most. And so, despite the turmoil, the essence of leadership remains unchanged.

It is not about submission to a single voice, but the courage to stand for something *greater than oneself*.

for political leaders to lead with not only their intellect and authority but also with their hearts. A vision that transforms the daunting challenges of our age into stepping stones towards a future where net zero is not the end goal, but the foundation upon which a thriving, inclusive society is built.

In this final chapter, as the narrative of our shared journey comes to a close, we are reminded that the future is ours to shape. It is a future where every decision, every policy, and every act of leadership is an affirmation of our commitment to one another. A future where caring for the environment is synonymous with caring for our communities, where sustainable development is the measure of progress, and where the net zero imperative serves as a beacon guiding us towards a more compassionate and just world.

May we all, leaders and citizens alike, draw inspiration from the challenges we face, and may we approach the monumental task of reimagining our world with a spirit of collaboration, empathy, and undying hope. The endeavour to achieve net zero is not merely a technical adjustment or an economic strategy - it is a profound statement of our values, a declaration that our collective future will be one defined by care, inclusivity, and the relentless pursuit of justice.

In closing, let this be a testament to the power of unified, compassionate leadership. Let it serve as a reminder that in the quest for a sustainable future, every voice matters, every act of care is significant, and every leader has a critical role to play. The journey to net zero is our shared responsibility, our common challenge, and, ultimately, our greatest opportunity to create a world that honours the best of who we are.

Epilogue

As I complete this book, the world's political landscape seems to drift further from the principles of true leadership. In one of the world's most influential democracies, dark rhetoric drowns out reason, diplomacy is cast aside, and those entrusted with power serve not the people, but a figure elevated beyond question. Integrity is no longer a virtue but an inconvenience, and authoritarianism is met not with resistance, but with reward.

How, then, can we still speak of leadership, integrity, and service? Because true leadership is not defined by those who betray it, but by those who uphold it against all odds. It is found in those who refuse to surrender their principles, who challenge deception with truth, and who understand that power is a duty, not a privilege.

History does not remember the sycophants – it remembers those who stood firm when it mattered most. And so, despite the turmoil, the essence of leadership remains unchanged.

It is not about submission to a single voice, but the courage to stand for something *greater than oneself*.

www.ingramcontent.com/pod-product-compliance
Lightning Source LLC
Chambersburg PA
CBHW011147290426
44109CB00023B/2524